Kids' Guide to the
INTERNET

Kids' Guide to the
INTERNET

by Bruce Goldstone and Arthur Perley
Illustrated by Dan Regan

Troll

Table of Contents

Chapter 1 What Is the Internet?   7

Chapter 2 A Key Pals' Tour of the Internet   13

Chapter 3 Getting Onto the Internet   23

Chapter 4 The ABCs of E-Mail   33

Chapter 5 The Talking Keyboard:
Chatting by Computer   45

Chapter 6 Welcome to the
World Wide Web   53

Chapter 7 Crawling Around the
World Wide Web   60

Chapter 8 Five Fantastic
Web Sites for Starters   75

Chapter 9 Web Wildlife:
An Explorer's Guide   86

Chapter 10 Armadillos on the Internet:
A Research Project Case Study   101

Chapter 11 Playing in MUDs   111

Chapter 12 Even More Cool Stuff
on the Net   118

Glossary   123

Index   126

Chapter 1

What Is the Internet?

You've read about it. You've heard other people talk about it. You're even reading this book about it. But what is it? What *is* the Internet?

Glad you asked! The Internet is an interconnected computer network. So what's that? Think about a giant, invisible system of highways connecting your computer to other computers around the world. But cars don't travel on this highway system—information does.

The Internet (many people call it just "the Net") is also known as the *information superhighway*. Big deal, you may be thinking. What's so terrific about information? "Information is just numbers and words," you might say. "It's a big bore." Oh, yeah? Well, here are just a few of the many kinds of information that can travel on the Internet:

- a letter you write to a friend in Australia
- a picture that shows what the world looks like to a bee
- a story about a third-grader who gets trapped inside her computer
- a video of a volcano blasting lava
- the sound of a moose sneezing

You see, almost anything you can think of can be considered information.

Computers are terrific tools because they can store information electronically. Your home or school computer can hold lots of information. So why do you need the Internet? Because there's a limit to how much information any one computer can hold. What happens if you run out of storage space on your computer? You have to erase something to add new information. Otherwise, you're stuck.

But what if you're using the Internet? Then you can get to the information stored on *other* computers, even if those computers are thousands of miles away. You can also send your own information anywhere in the world, to anyone who uses the Internet. The Internet makes it possible for you to hook up to millions and millions of other computers. Right now there are about 40 million computers on the Internet!

Your on-line adventures are about to begin. *On-line* is the term used to describe anything that happens when your computer is hooked up to a computer network. Hop in front of your monitor and get ready to ride the information superhighway. Don't know where you're going? Relax. That's what the rest of this book is all about.

To get on the Internet, your computer calls up another computer that is already part of the Internet. Once connected, your computer automatically becomes part of this giant network.

What Isn't the Internet?

Before we go any further, let's clear up some common misunderstandings kids have about the Internet.

• The Internet is *not* free. Signing on almost always costs money, so make sure that you have permission to sign on before you start.

• The Internet is not a video game. Okay, you *can* play games on the Internet. But you can do a whole lot more than that.

• The Internet is not a breakfast cereal. (Not yet, anyway!)

RULES FOR INTERNET TRAVELERS

Any traveler needs to follow safety rules. If you take a car trip, you need to fasten your seat belt, and the driver must obey traffic signals. If you fly on a plane, you need to know how to leave the plane safely in an emergency.

People who travel on the Internet—Net "surfers"—also follow special rules. These rules can help you explore the exciting resources of the Internet without putting yourself at risk.

1. _NEVER give out personal information._ Remember that the people you talk to on the Internet are strangers. You don't really know anything much about them. Most people you meet on the Internet are honest, but some people lie about themselves and may have less than honorable motives for talking to you.

So when you meet anyone on the Internet, remember not to tell them anything too personal. Here's a list of some things you should never give out over the Internet:

- **your phone number**
- **your address**
- **your password**
- **your photo**

2. _Don't arrange off-line meetings._ Remember, you don't know the person on the other computer. It's just not wise to plan a meeting with people you've met only through the Internet, even if they become good friends.

Lots of kids have friends on the Internet whom they never meet. There are even some advantages to Internet friendships. For one thing, you never have to worry about your hair or what you're wearing!

If you can't _live_ without meeting a great new Internet friend, or at least calling that friend on the phone, make sure that you tell an adult first.

3. Go with your instincts. Your feelings are often your best guide to personal safety. If someone sends you e-mail or messages that make you feel uncomfortable, don't write back. Save any weird or upsetting messages you get and show them to an adult.

4. Be patient. Getting information on the Internet can be slow. Sometimes it feels like you're waiting forever to get a picture. Remember that information may be traveling thousands and thousands of miles to get to your computer. A lot of Net surfers keep a notebook at the computer so that they can write or draw while they're waiting.

5. Set time limits. Time really flies when you're having fun, and the Internet can sure be a lot of fun. Unfortunately, it's not free. It's easy to forget about time while you're surfing the Net. Here's one all-too-familiar situation: You sign on at noon just to see if you got any messages. You read your mail and spend awhile writing back. Then you decide to read an on-line magazine, which gives you a great idea that you really want to share in an on-line conversation. The next thing you know, it's time for dinner, and you've been on-line for hours. Well, we don't want to be there when your family gets the bill!

The best way to avoid problems like this is to set up a budget. Talk with your family about how much time you can spend each week on the Internet. Then, before signing on, set yourself a specific time limit. Write down the time you sign on so that you don't forget it. When your time's up, *sign off!* Well, okay, if you're in a really great conversation, you can stay on-line a little bit longer. Just don't get carried away.

6. Respect your on-line friends. Treat people on-line the same way you treat people you're with in person. That means not being insulting or using foul language. Sometimes kids get carried away when they're typing at their computer and say mean things that can hurt other people's feelings. Remember, on-line conversations are just as real as any others.

Basically, follow the old rule: Treat other people the way you want to be treated. It works when you meet people at school, and it works when you meet people on the Internet, too.

RIPs AND UBIs

As you read this book, you'll find that two special symbols show up from time to time.

When you see this sign, read carefully! We're drawing your attention to a *Really Important Point!*

This sign, on the other hand, means that we're telling you something interesting but not critical. These are facts we thought you might like to know because they're fun or just plain weird. We put a lava lamp on the sign because we couldn't think of anything less useful.

Chapter 2

A Key Pals' Tour of the Internet

Anna, Yoshi, Jenny, and Homer are all good friends, but they've never met! Well, they've never met in person, anyway. They all met each other on the Internet.

When you write letters to someone in another state or country, you and the person you write to are *pen pals*. Anna says that she and her Internet friends are *key pals*, since they use their computer keyboards to talk to each other.

Right now all four friends are sitting in front of their computers, ready to start another exciting Internet adventure. This chapter will give you a good idea of some of the things you can do on the Internet.

13

SIGNING ON

Everyone has a special name when they are on-line. Yoshi uses the name TokyoRacer. Anna uses the name Anna10. Your on-line name is called your *user ID*.

The first thing you need to know about the Internet is how to get there. There's more than one way to sign on. In fact, each of our key pals uses a different way to get onto the Internet.

Anna has a Macintosh computer at home. Anna's family decided to use a service named America Online to get onto the Internet. They compared the different services and decided that America Online was best for them.

When Anna's family registered, America Online sent them a floppy disk. Anna's family carefully followed the directions for installing the program disk on their own computer. It's now stored on their computer's hard drive. They use the program by just clicking on the America Online *icon*, a small picture that stays on their desktop.

When Anna clicks on the icon, she sees a sign-on screen. She picks her user ID from this list:

Each name represents a person in Anna's family who uses America Online. *MTJuarez* is Anna's mom, *JJuarez* is her dad, *Anna10* is Anna, and *Zoomer888* is her brother. Anna picked the name *Anna10* because she was ten years old when she started using the Internet. Now she's 11, but she doesn't want to change her ID because everyone knows it already.

After picking her name, Anna types in her secret password. She's the only one who knows her password. Then she uses her mouse to click on a "button" that appears on her screen, and the computer dials a telephone number. She hears sounds like a push-button phone makes and then an irritating *SKREEKKKEKKKKCCH* noise. That's the sound of her computer hooking up with another computer.

In just a few seconds, Anna's connected to America Online. To get to the Internet, all she has to do is click on another button labeled *Internet Connection.*

At his house Homer has an IBM-compatible computer. His family decided to use a service called CompuServe. Even though this service is different from Anna's, signing on is pretty much the same.

Homer finds his user ID, Cyclops, and types in his secret password. Then he clicks on a button and connects to CompuServe. One more quick click and he's on the Internet.

Yoshi and Jenny use computers at their school computer labs. Each school uses a different program to get to the Internet. Even though they use different programs, Yoshi and Jenny still have to pick their user IDs and then type in their passwords.

For more information about signing on to the Internet, see Chapter 3.

E-MAIL

The first thing Yoshi wants to do on the Internet is send a note to Anna. Letters and notes that you send through your computer are called *e-mail*. That's short for *electronic mail*.

Yoshi writes this letter:

```
To: Anna10
From: TokyoRacer
Subject: Hi from Japan

    Hi, Anna. My mother says I can
only stay on-line for 30
minutes today. It's not enough
time!!!! I have so many things
to do. I have a lot of
schoolwork, too. Did you get an
e-mail note from Homer? He's
the funniest key pal I know.
    I'm going to try to visit the
Kid's Com chat line on Saturday
at 9 PM. If you sign on at 7 AM, we
can talk live! Is that too early
for you?

    Bye for now,
    Yoshi
```

When Anna signs on, her computer flashes a message. She has mail! She looks in her "inbox" and finds Yoshi's letter. To send a note back, she just clicks on a button and types her message back:

```
To: TokyoRacer
From: Anna1D
Subject: 7 AM?!

    7 AM? UGH! Saturday is my one day
to sleep late. Can we make it 7:3D,
anyway? I'll be more fun to talk to
if I'm awake.
    Talk to you soon,
    Bye,
    Anna ;)
```

For more information about sending e-mail, turn to Chapter 4.

CHAT ROOMS

Jenny loves to talk with kids from around the world. As soon as she signs on, she checks for e-mail. Then she goes straight to her favorite chat rooms. Today, she decides to see who's at The Stoop.

When she gets there, she sees a list of 23 names. That means that 23 people are on-line at exactly the same time. They are sitting at computers in San Francisco, Honolulu, London, and other cities, big and small.

To add her own comments, Jenny just types in what she wants to say and hits the Return key. Her comments show up on the computer screen next to her user ID. Jenny's user ID is JenGenius.

Jenny wants to make some new key pals today. Here's a quick sample of the chat Jen takes part in:

```
    JenGenius: Helloooo from
Honolulu!
    KTLyler: Greeting, earthlings.
I'm from the planet Xorax.
    Pablo89: Yeah, and I'm a giant
penguin.
    Emil2U: It's snowing here in
Maine, but not hard enough to
cancel school.  :(
    Pablo89: I bet they never cancel
school for snow in Honolulu, eh,
Jen?
```

```
    JenGenius: No, but if it's
really nice, we get a SUN day and
everyone runs amok outdoors. ;-)
    1DERFUL: I wish I were in
Hawaii. It sounds terrific.
    KTLyler: Xorax has three suns
and 1,000 moons!
    JenGenius: You're right, it is
pretty 1DERFUL here in Honolulu!
```

The chat room Jenny visited was open to kids who wanted to talk about anything. Chat room conversation can change a lot when a new person comes into the "room." Some chat rooms have special topics, such as sports, movies, or pets. You might even find a chat room where people will help you with your math homework.

You'll find more information about finding and talking in chat rooms in Chapter 5.

THE WORLD WIDE WEB

Homer decides that today he's going to explore the World Wide Web. The Web is sort of like a giant library or magazine stand your computer can take you to. In just half an hour of Web surfing, you can visit an amazing variety of people, places, and things.

Here's a quick tour of the places Homer visits today. His trip starts with a visit to the White House in Washington, D.C., where he reads about the building's history and the current first family. He even sees pictures of their pets!

Next, Homer decides to explore what the Web has to say about his new favorite sport: in-line skating. Homer knows that you can look up just about anything on the World Wide Web. He uses a *search service*, which is like an index to the Web. All he has to do is type in the phrase *in-line skates*, and he gets a list of different Web pages that talk about this topic.

Here are a few of the things Homer finds:

- In-line skating publications, such as *XSK8 Magazine, In-Line,* and *Skatermag.* Each magazine has articles, pictures, and sometimes even videos.

- Descriptions of in-line skating in different parts of the world. Homer reads about skating in New York City, the Netherlands, Philadelphia, Vienna, and Santa Barbara.

- Profiles of skating teams in Boston, New York, New Mexico, and Washington, D.C. Homer finds out team members' names and what skates they wear. He even sees photos of their favorite moves.

- Descriptions and pictures of products for sale. Homer knows that some Web pages are like commercials. You can't believe everything you read, even on the World Wide Web.

- Information about roller hockey teams, equipment, and rules.

Before he signs off the Internet, Homer checks out one last Web feature. He goes to the World Wide Web Fortune Cookie Machine to get a random fortune for the day. Today his fortune is, "It's better to think without talking than talk without thinking."

Chapters 6 to 9 tell you more about the World Wide Web.

MUDs AND OTHER GAMES

After she finishes writing to her friend TokyoRacer, Anna decides it's time for a game. She decides to play Manic Maze. All she has to do is type in the game's "address" on her computer and press the Enter key. Her computer searches for the game at this address.

Manic Maze is just one of thousands of different games on the Internet. Anna likes this game because it's challenging but doesn't take too long to play.

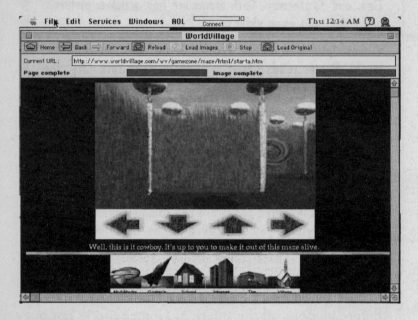

There are Internet games to match every interest. You can play word games, logic puzzles, or arcade shoot-outs, or even go on an Internet treasure hunt. You can also enter brilliantly complex "worlds" called MUDs (multiuser dungeons) that are similar to role-playing games.

Check out Chapter 11 for more information about playing games on the Internet.

Chapter 3

Getting Onto the Internet

Okay, you know that the Internet is a worldwide network of computers. You've seen some things you can do on the Net. Now you want to get started. But how do you get to the Internet? Well, you'll need three things to get there:

> • a computer •a modem •software

A *modem* is like a telephone for your computer. *Software* programs tell the computer what to do, such as open a window on a screen or make a sound.

Computers use modems to call other computers. Remember the *SKREEKKCCH* noise Anna heard when she signed on? That was the sound of her computer talking to another computer.

Computers talking to each other? Isn't that impossible? And how can a computer in France understand a computer in the United States, anyway?

Well, computers don't talk to each other the same way you and I do. They use a special language—we'll call it *computerese*. All computers on the Internet speak computerese.

INTERNET PROVIDERS AND ON-LINE SERVICES

One way to get your computer hooked up to the Internet is through your *Internet Service Provider (ISP)*. ISPs are companies that connect computers to the Internet, just as telephone companies connect telephones. Some ISPs are big, like the big telephone companies, while others are small local businesses.

Many people use on-line services such as America Online, CompuServe, or Prodigy to hook up to the Internet. An on-line service is different from an ISP. An on-line service is a private computer network that you pay money to use. Each on-line service has special features available only to its users. Although you can get to the Internet using an on-line service, some parts will not be accessible.

So why do people use on-line services? Well, they're often easier to use than ISPs.

On-line services became popular when the Internet was young and very complicated. A person used to have to be a real computer whiz to figure it out.

On-line services make it easy to send e-mail, meet people through your computer, and do some other things. But today the Internet is easier to use, and anybody can get directly to the Internet and connect with the rest of the world.

Choosing an ISP can be difficult. You have to know how much it costs and how to set up your computer for an Internet connection. You have to know what sort of modem you have and what sorts of things—such as memory and hard disks—are in your computer. Unless you already have one, your family or teachers should help pick out an ISP for you to use.

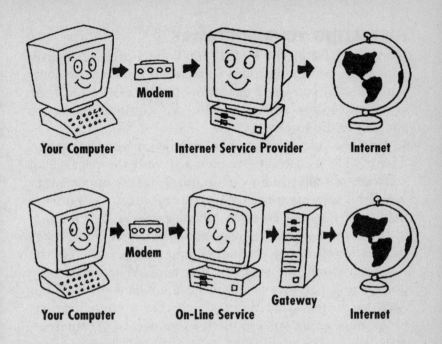

Your Computer   Internet Service Provider   Internet

Your Computer   On-Line Service   Gateway   Internet

An Internet Service Provider hooks you up directly to the Internet. An on-line service can hook you up to the Internet, too, but it goes through an Internet "gateway." This gateway may not let all available information through.

Useless But Interesting

Using the Internet used to be difficult because it wasn't designed with everyday users in mind. Originally a military computer network, *ARPAnet* changed its name in 1969 to *Internet*. But it had been designed for computer experts and remained very hard to use until the 1990s. By then, so many people were interested in using the Internet that something had to change—and it did. Today, thanks to programmers, the Internet is a lot easier to use and should continue to improve!

INSTALLING YOUR SOFTWARE

Once you have picked an ISP, you'll get a package of disks containing communications software to use on your computer, just as you get a disk from an on-line service. The communications software tells the computer how to connect to the Internet.

First the software has to be installed in your computer. There will be instructions included with the package of software that tell you how to do this. It is very important to install this software correctly. If you're unsure, try to get some help or let someone else with more experience do it for you.

Anna and her parents installed an America Online communications program on their computer. They inserted the floppy disk and followed the directions. When they were done, the program was stored on their hard drive. You'll need to do the same thing. Once your communications program is set up, you can use it to connect to the Internet.

CONNECTING

Once you've got the software installed, you're ready to go on the Internet! The first step to getting on the Internet is making the connection. You tell your computer to make the connection by running your Internet communications program.

When you hear all that screeching and whistling, your computer is linking to the Internet. You're almost there. But there's one other thing you need to do before you are officially on-line. You have to tell the Internet computer who you are.

Hi, I'm Mike!

CHOOSING YOUR USER ID

How does the Internet computer know that you're you? *You* know who you are. You just look in the mirror and say, "That's me!" If someone far away needs to know what you look like, you can give them a picture. But the Internet computer can't see you, so you need another way of being identified on the Internet.

When you connect to the Internet computer, you'll see a box on the screen where you will have to fill in your user ID and password. Your user ID is the name you use on the Internet. This is how other Internet people will know you. It's how they will send you mail and chat with you. Your user ID is your Internet nickname, and you can make it whatever you want it to be. Use a name from a favorite story or cartoon, or maybe make up a name. You can be anyone you want to be on the Internet—an astronaut or a sorcerer, a hero or a monster. It's up to you.

You might not be able to get your first choice for user ID. If someone else has already taken the name you want, you'll have to choose another. Try to think of a few backup ideas. Your user ID can't be too long, either. The limit varies, but it's a good idea to choose a name that's no more than ten characters in total.

Here are some sample user IDs. What does each make you think of? What would you like your ID to say about you?

PBJ44120   PigsRQTs

Karin12345   BigZoid12

HorseLvr   PieFace10

JUMPITUP   Agent99

Wizzard   RoyDConn

ImYrFrnd   LDeanLDean

TBaker400   LLemming

HannaH   Internut

JuneBday   PabloP

Some people think that a user ID shouldn't be too personal. For example, John decided to use this user ID: John12inLA. He picked the name because his name is John, he's 12 years old, and he lives in Los Angeles. That's a lot of information to give out to strangers right away. A lot of kids like to choose a name that's more mysterious, like ZWalrus or One4All. Then you can decide when to share personal information, such your name, age, or where you live. (City only, please. And NEVER give out your street address.)

Remember, once you've picked out a name, you're stuck with it. You can't easily change it if you get tired of it, so pick a name you like and stick with it.

PICKING YOUR PASSWORD

After your user ID is *input*—typed in or selected from a list on your sign-on screen—you type in your secret password. Your password is like your own personal key that unlocks the Internet door and allows you to go onto the Internet.

You choose a password at the same time as you choose your user ID. Make up a password that is easy for you to remember. Write it down and keep it in a safe place, or give it to someone in your family or a teacher to keep for you. You will need to input your user ID and password every time you sign on.

Choose your password carefully! Don't pick one that's easy to figure out, such as your name, your user ID, or your phone number. Try to think of something that's easy to remember but not too obvious.

Also, if you write your password down to remember it, don't write "Internet password: bicycle" on a notecard. Just write "bicycle." You'll remember what the word is, but no one else who finds the paper will make the connection.

Once the Internet computer recognizes your user ID and password, you're on the Internet for real! The door to this great big worldwide network is now open. Chat with someone in Japan, see a brand-new picture of Jupiter, listen to an avalanche, or send e-mail to someone's cat! Go for it—it's all out there for you!

THE INTERNET PROTOCOL

The Internet computers now know you by your user ID. But how do the Internet computers know each other? After all, they all look pretty much alike! Well, every computer on the Internet has what is called an *IP address*. IP stands for *Internet Protocol*—big words that mean, "How we do things on the Internet."

All the things you do on the Internet—from sending e-mail, playing games, and chatting with a friend to looking for dinosaurs—have to follow the Internet rules. The Internet Protocol is the set of all the rules for all the computers on the Internet. These rules are built into the programs that you use when you're on the Internet. The rules include a set of numbers that make up computer "addresses." Think about your telephone number. It is a set of numbers that identifies your home. A computer address is a set of numbers that identifies a computer. Whenever your computer sends a message, it includes its own address. Computers tell each other apart by reading each other's Internet address.

GETTING FROM A TO B

How does information move around on the Internet? Well, suppose you want to look at a picture of a dinosaur. Compare the way a picture might get passed in a classroom with how it is done on the Internet.

In a Classroom	On the Internet
Katy has a picture of a dinosaur. Max wants to see it. But the teacher is talking. What can Max do?	A great dinosaur picture is stored on a computer in Germany. Max wants to see it. How can Max see the picture?
Max writes a note!	Max clicks on SEE PICTURE on a Web page. That tells his computer to write a note.
Max passes the note to Shandra.	Max's computer passes the request to a computer in Chicago.
Shandra passes the note to Leon.	The Chicago computer passes the request to a computer in London.
Leon passes the note to Katy.	The request arrives at the computer in Germany.
Katy agrees, and sends the picture back along the same route.	The computer analyzes the request and sends the picture (in digital form, of course) back along the same route.

Computers passing messages and connecting—this is how the Internet works. All the things that you do on the Internet connect you to other computers. So, really, the Internet is just a bunch of computers playing catch! They all know each other's Internet address, so everything ends up in the right place. And all the computers on the Internet are passing messages and pictures and sounds and movies and other things from users all day long, every single day. The Internet is a very, very busy place!

So that's how you connect to the Internet! Once you do it a few times, it won't take very long. It will be like using the telephone or turning on the TV—*really* easy! In the next two chapters you'll find out how to send someone an electronic letter through the Internet and how to "talk" with other people on the Internet using your keyboard.

Chapter 4

The ABCs of E-Mail

One of the first things that most kids want to do when they get on-line is write letters to other kids. It's fast, easy, and fun. This chapter will show you how to send and receive electronic notes from your own key pals.

E-mail, as you know, is *electronic mail*. You can use it for any kind of letter or note you want to send to someone else on the Internet. That means *anyone* else—users in India, Peru, or Podunk are just a mouse click away.

WHY E-MAIL?

E-mail has some advantages over regular mail. Consider these terrific features:

- E-mail travels immediately.
- E-mail is cheap. Even a long letter won't take very long to send.
- E-mail can be sent at any time. Unlike letters from the post office, e-mail can be sent or received 24 hours a day.
- E-mail is great for sending quick notes, too. Because it's so easy, many kids send short e-mail notes rather than long letters. If they forget something important, it's easy enough to send another e-mail note.

E-mail is cheap to send, but writing your e-mail notes can take a while. Smart users write their notes *before* they sign on to the Internet. Then they pay only for the time it actually takes to send the message.

ANATOMY OF AN E-MAIL ADDRESS

How does your letter carrier know where to deliver your mail? By looking at the address on the envelope, of course. So how does the Internet know where to deliver your e-mail? By looking at the e-mail address you give it.

Every Internet user has a personal e-mail address. An e-mail address is similar to a post office box. When an e-mail message is sent, a computer looks at the address to decide which user gets the mail.

All e-mail addresses follow a specific format. Just as your home address includes your name, street address, city, state, and zip code, an e-mail address has specific parts.

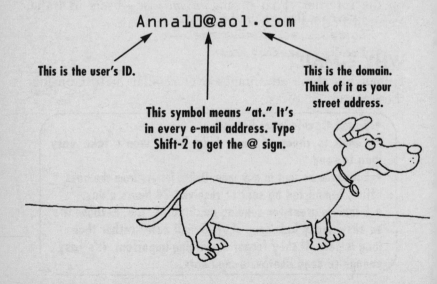

`Anna10@aol.com`

This is the user's ID.

This symbol means "at." It's in every e-mail address. Type Shift-2 to get the @ sign.

This is the domain. Think of it as your street address.

E-mail addresses have to be exactly right. Pay careful attention when you give your address to someone or type someone's address on the computer. If you make a mistake in an address, the Internet won't know where to find the person you want to write to. Here are some hints.

E-mail addresses should:
- never have any spaces in them
- have one, and only one, @ sign

Every e-mail address has two parts: the user ID and the *domain*. The parts are separated by an @ ("at") sign. The domain part of the address identifies the computer site—where it is and what kind of place it is. Some parts of the domain will make sense to you; some parts will look like computer gibberish. You can try to read the domain for hints about the address. For example, each on-line service has a specific domain, such as:

- **America Online: aol.com**
- **CompuServe: compuserve.com**
- **Prodigy: prodigy.com**

The last three letters of many e-mail addresses also give you hints about the address. If you read these letters, you may be able to figure out something about the kind of computer connection someone has. Here are seven common domains:

- **edu:** educational sites, such as schools and colleges
- **com:** commercial sites, including commercial Internet providers (such as America Online and CompuServe) and big companies (such as Warner Brothers or Mattel)
- **gov:** government sites, such as the White House
- **mil:** military sites
- **net:** network sites
- **org:** organization sites (These are noncommercial sites.)
- **int:** international sites

Some domains are longer than others. Here's another example of an e-mail address:

PinBot@bronze.ucs.indiana.edu

If you look closely at PinBot's e-mail address, you'll be able to guess that PinBot uses a computer at a school site because of the *edu* at the end. What state university might PinBot be connected with?

Now that you know all about domains, we should tell you that people with on-line services often don't need them. If you're using an on-line service, you don't need to use the domain if you're sending e-mail to someone else on the same service. For example, Isaac uses Prodigy, and his user ID is Casai99. Cleo, too, uses Prodigy. If she wants to write to Isaac, she just types "Casai99" in the address box. Thomas uses a different Internet provider. If he wants to write to Isaac, he needs to use the whole address:

Casai99@prodigy.com

YOUR FIRST E-MAIL MESSAGE

All right, you have your user ID and you know something about e-mail. It's time to e-mail a letter. In this exercise you'll create an e-mail letter and send it to us at *Kids' Guide*. We'll turn right around and send you e-mail back! Okay, here we go!

First go to your menu and open your e-mail program. You may see *Compose Mail* or *New Message*. That's the place to start. You'll get a screen similar to the one below:

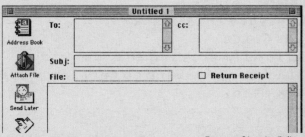

Courtesy of America Online

The parts are pretty simple:

• **To.**   This is where you type the e-mail address of the person you're sending mail to. You can put more than one name here if you're going to send the same e-mail to more than one person. You might use it to send birthday party invitations to friends or mail a funny picture to a bunch of your relatives.

• **From.**   Your user ID is already in the program. When you send your e-mail, your ID will automatically appear at the top of the note.

• **CC.**   This is where you put the address of anyone you want to send a *carbon copy* of your message to. In practice it gives you another way to send e-mail to more than one person. Just type in the e-mail addresses of other people you want to receive your note.

• **Subject.**   This space is for the title of your e-mail letter. All e-mail should include a subject description. The description makes it easier to find your mail in your mail folder.

You write your letter in the part of the e-mail screen called the *body*. This comes after the *header*—the address and subject information. You have to fill out the header correctly, or the e-mail won't go out.

Here's how to fill out an e-mail note to us at *Kids' Guide:*

To: KidsGuide@bigmagic.com
From: <this is where your user ID is>
Subject: Hello
CC: <leave this blank>
Kids Guide,
Hello, I'm writing an e-mail to you! I look forward to getting one back, too.

Write anything you want here!

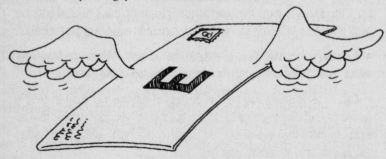

Now click on the Send button, and off goes your mail! That's all there is to it. If you have a problem, don't panic. It's probably just a spelling error or something simple. Good luck, and thanks for the e-mail!

QUICK RESPONSE

When you get e-mail and want to respond right away, do it the easy way—click on an option called *Reply*. The Reply option will automatically set up a new letter for you. It will already have the *To:* address filled in with the address of the person who wrote to you. Just type a response in the body of the letter and click on Send. That's it!

SAVING YOUR MAIL

All of your e-mail will be saved in the in-box of your e-mail program. It will stay there forever unless you move it. If you don't move your mail to folders you've set up in your e-mail program, your inbox will get pretty crowded.

You create a new mailbox folder using your e-mail program, naming it "Bobby's Mail" (if your name is Bobby!) or "Personal" or something like that. You can make other folders, too, for particular things: one for school, one for sports—anything you like. Move your e-mail to these folders after you've read the messages and responded. Cleaning up is important on computers, too.

It's also a good idea to weed out your e-mail files once in a while. Do you really need that note from three months ago about Ellen's birthday party? If not, delete it.

If you use an on-line service, you will collect e-mail in a slightly different way. Your mail will probably be stored with the service, not on your computer. You can read it, but it will disappear after a few days if you don't save it. If you get a note you want to keep, choose Save. Then you can save the e-mail on your hard drive or a floppy disk.

MAILING MORE THAN JUST WORDS

Do you use a computer paint program, such as Kid Pix or MacDraw? Suppose you did a drawing you really liked and wanted to show it to a key pal. Most e-mail programs will let you send computer files along with your e-mail note. This is called *attaching a file*.

Here are a few kinds of files you can attach to your e-mail note:

- **computer drawings and pictures**
- **wacky sounds**
- **games**
- **photographs (usually saved in special formats).**

Every e-mail program is slightly different. Check your manual or on-line Help to find out how to attach files.

KEEPING TRACK OF YOUR FRIENDS

Even though e-mail addresses are shorter than most home addresses, they're still pretty hard to remember. All of those periods, numbers, and abbreviations just don't stick in the mind very well. That's why e-mail programs let you set up a *personal address book*.

You should keep an address book for your key pals. In most e-mail programs, all you have to do is select the address book from the menu. To make an entry, just type in the person's user ID and e-mail address. If you know the person's real name, you'll probably want to add that, too.

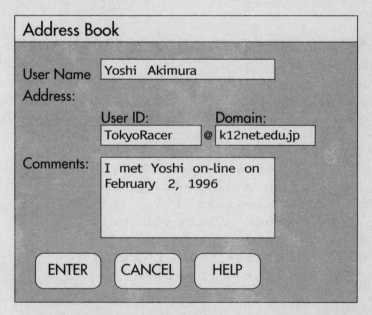

There's another big advantage to using an address book. It gets you out of typing those long, annoying e-mail addresses! Just open your address book and highlight the address you want. Then click on OK or cut and paste the address to use it in a new piece of e-mail!

SMILEYS AND OTHER KINDS OF SHORTHAND

You've seen a few *smileys* in this book already. They're those funny-looking punctuation marks at the end of some on-line messages. You might want to use smileys in your e-mail and your on-line chats. Look at this chat between two key pals:

```
    Lars11: I can't sign on
tomorrow. I have to go to
piano lessons. :-(
    Cr8er: Maybe you could
lose your piano books. ;-)
    Lars11: Yeah, if I want my
mom to yell at me. :-P
```

The trick to reading a smiley is to look at it from the side. You should see something that looks sort of like a face.

Putting a smiley at the end of a sentence lets people know how you're feeling. Smileys come in handy when you want to show that you're making a joke or a sarcastic remark.

There are lots and lots of smileys. Kids come up with new faces all the time. This chart shows some of the smileys you'll see and use a lot, but try to invent your own, too!

:-)	smiling
;-)	winking and smiling (good for sarcastic or flirty comments)
:-(	frowning
:-C	really frowning
:-P	sticking out your tongue
:-D	laughing
:'-(	crying
:-I	bored
:-O	amazed
:-*	a kiss
<:-)	smiling in a dunce cap
#:-)	smiling with messy hair
=(:-o)	frightened/hair standing on end
:-{>	smiling with a mustache and beard
8-)	smiling wearing sunglasses

Some kids use abbreviations that save them from typing lots of letters. A few abbreviations show up a lot. This chart lists some of the most common abbreviations:

ADN	any day now
ASAP	as soon as possible
B4N	bye for now
BBS	bulletin board system
BL	belly laughing
BRB	be right back
BTA	but then again
BTW	by the way

CU	see you
CUL	see you later
F2F	face to face
FAQ	frequently asked question
FWIW	for what it's worth
FYI	for your information
GAL	get a life
GIWIST	Gee, I wish I'd said that.
GMTA	Great minds think alike.
IC	I see
ILY	I love you.
IMHO	in my humble opinion
IOW	in other words
JIC	just in case
JK	just kidding
L8R	later
LOL	laughing out loud
OTOH	on the other hand
POV	point of view
RPG	role-playing games
S/AC	sex/age check
Txs	thanks
WFM	works for me
WYSIWYG	What you see is what you get.

There are some other shorthand tricks kids use on-line, too:

{JenGenius}	Writing someone's name in curly brackets means you're giving them a hug.
{{{{JenGenius}}}}	Extra curly brackets mean an extra-big hug.
<g>	A g within angle brackets means a grin.

Chapter 5

The Talking Keyboard: Chatting by Computer

E-mail is a terrific way to send notes to people you already know. But how can you find new friends on the Internet? Go to an Internet chat room.

A *chat room* (sometimes called a *chat line*) isn't a real room. It isn't even a real place. It's just an electronic connection between people sitting at home, in school, or anywhere else they might have computers. When you enter a chat room, you are instantly hooked up with other people in the same room. You send messages to other people in the room by typing on your keyboard.

You might think of a chat room as a telephone connection between a lot of people, except that instead of using your voice to talk, you use your keyboard.

EXCITING, CONFUSING, OR JUST PLAIN WEIRD

The conversations in chat rooms can go pretty fast. Imagine 20 or more people all talking at the same time! Words and ideas fly by, new people come and go, and grammar and spelling rules go out the window. Things can get pretty confusing, even if you're one of the people talking.

These pages show a sample chat room conversation. Don't worry if some of it seems confusing. Most of the people talking were probably a little confused, too!

```
〖SERVER〗   Aimee444 has entered the room.
Aimee444    hi, everybody.
BabarFan    hi, Aimee!!!!
Fifty5      HELLO
CrawlieZ    Jana: r u playing soccer
            tomorrow?
Linkster    welcome, Aimeeeeeeee :-)
MiguelP     I SHOULD BE DOING MY HOMEWORK
JanaJana    CrawlieZ: no, I have to go to
            the dentist :-C
PitaBread   anyone else here a Virgo?
IgtheOg     I found a bug in my pbj
            sandwich today
Fifty5      yuck
BabarFan    EEEEeeeeeewwwwww!!!!
John938     did you eat it anyway?
Shauna      :-P
MiguelP     I HATE THE DENTIST
CrawlieZ    Pita: I'm a Virgo
Zotox       I have a pet tarantula
```

```
Igthe0g    what does he eat?
JanaJana   my dentist eats food like
               anybody else
Linkster   I might play socer tomorrow
Igthe0g    not your dentist - the tarantula
Wiggles    Blech!
Zotox      he eats dentists!!!!
Fifty5     yeah, right
Shauna     LOL
Zotox      IMHO tarantullas are great pets
John938    IMNSHO spiders are GROSS
[SERVER]   LillyPad has entered the room.
CrawlieZ   no way
Wiggles    whats IMNSHO?
LillyPad   ><     ><
MiguelP    I HATE SPIDERS
BabarFan   Lilly: nice fish
John938    in my not so humbel opinion
Igthe0g    Miguel: STOP SHOUTING!!!
JanaJana   I have to go check my mail BRB
[SERVER]   JanaJana has left the room.
```

As you can see, on-line chats can be pretty confusing. Once things are really rolling, comments fly by pretty fast. But don't worry. You'll get used to reading messages in chat rooms. It's almost like learning another language. Luckily, it's not a very hard language. Kids around the world have gotten used to it, and we're sure you can, too. Just try to be patient. And ask questions if you don't understand something.

THE BASICS OF ON-LINE CHAT ROOMS

There are lots of chat rooms designed for kids. These rooms are meant to be safe places where kids can exchange ideas, jokes, and whatever strange thoughts pop into their minds. Some chat rooms are monitored by an adult guide. A monitor makes sure that people act properly and follow the rules.

On-line services such as America Online and Prodigy have their own special chat rooms and areas for kids. Lots of kids use these rooms instead of Internet chat rooms because they're easy to find and are usually monitored.

On-line chatting is one of the fastest ways to lose track of time on the Internet. It's a good idea to set a time limit *before* you enter a chat room. When your time's up, *leave*. Don't say, "Just another five minutes," because the next thing you know, it'll be five *hours* later.

Getting to a Chat Room

We've found a lot of terrific chat rooms on the World Wide Web. These rooms are monitored and are safe for kids. You'll learn a lot more about the World Wide Web in Chapters 6 to 9.

To get to a Web chat room, you'll need to sign onto the Internet. Follow the steps described in Chapter 3. Then use your *Web browser*. That's the program that tells your computer where to find the chat room. You'll need to know the address (URL—see p. 58) of the chat room.

These are the basic steps you'll follow to get to a Web chat room:

1. Sign onto the Internet.
2. Start using your Web browser (see Chapter 7).
3. Type the address of the chat room on the URL line of your Web browser.
4. Press Enter or Return on your keyboard.

Your Web browser will take you to the room you're looking for. Then just follow the instructions for the room. Some rooms will let your choose a name before you enter. This name could be your user ID, but it could be different, too.

Talking in a Chat Room

Sending a message in a chat room is really simple. Just type in your message and click on the Send button. In some rooms, this might also be called the Send Message button or the Reply button.

That's all there is to it! Your message will appear on the screen, next to your chat room name.

Most chat rooms also include a list of people in the room. You can scroll through the list to find out who you're talking to.

Netiquette Rules

When you're surfing the Net, you should always follow the safety rules described in Chapter 1. In particular, never give out personal information on-line. So don't give your full name and address in a chat room.

There are some special additional rules that people follow in chat rooms. Since social rules are sometimes called *etiquette*, Net surfers like to call these rules *netiquette*.

Here are a few netiquette rules:

• **Don't swear.** Curse words are rude and disrespectful. That goes for using symbols to mask the words, too. Swearing can really ruin an on-line chat, so don't do it.

• **No scrolling.** Scrolling is hitting the Return key again and again without writing a message. It adds a lot of blank space to the conversation and it's really annoying, so why do it?

• **Be considerate.** Remember, you're talking to real people with real feelings. Don't say things just to hurt or annoy other people.

• **Don't overuse CAPS (capital letters).** Typing in CAPS is like shouting on-line. Would you want to have a whole conversation shouting? Use caps only when you have something really important to say.

• **Try to stay on the topic.** If people are having a conversation about llamas, don't ask a question about zeppelins.

• **Protect your password.** Don't tell your password to anyone, and don't ask anyone for theirs.

Remembering Your New Key Pals

A lot of on-line conversations involve 20 or 30 people talking at a time. That's a lot of names to remember! If you get into a really good conversation, you might want to save it on your computer. That way, you can read it again whenever you want. You can also use the saved conversation to help you remember who you were talking to.

To save a chat room conversation:

1. Find the Save option on your browser menu.
2. Choose a folder or directory to put your conversation in.
3. Name the conversation. You might use a date (Feb697) or a topic (Spiders).
4. Then hit Enter or press OK to save the conversation.

SOME CHAT ROOMS TO CHECK OUT

Here's a list of some places on the World Wide Web that have chat areas for kids. Remember, to get to one of these, just type in the URL (the Web page address—see page 58) on the URL line in your Web browser. Then press Return. Your browser will take you there.

Kid's Com

URL: http://www.kids.com/

You'll need to register the first time you visit this chat room. Just answer the questions, then click on OK.

Kidlink

URL: http://www.kidlink.org/

You'll need to register to talk with Kidlink kids from around the world. Since Kidlink was started in 1990, over 50,000 kids from 80 countries have visited this Web site.

The On-Ramp's Chat Room for Kids

URL: http://www.theonramp.net:8002/join

Join this chat room to make new cyberfriends. The registration page will ask you for your personal URL—that's for kids who have their own home pages. But don't worry, you don't need a home page to join the conversation.

FOX Entertainment Chat Room

URL: http://www.foxnetwork.com/Prime/Chat/Transcripts/index.html

Chat live with your favorite stars from the FOX network. You can also visit this Web page to find out when the next chats will take place or read transcripts from past chats.

Sega Chat Room

URL: http://www.segaoa.com/live/chat/

This chat room is sponsored by Sega and offers nifty illustrations from Sega games that you can add to your messages.

Pre-Teen Chat Room at Web Broadcasting Service

URL: http://www.irsociety.com/cgi-bin/Webchat_doorway.cgi?Room=Pre-Teen_Chat

This room is part of a larger group of chat rooms. You might find other rooms at the Web Broadcasting Service that focus on your favorite topics.

Chapter 6

Welcome to the World Wide Web

Okay, you've sent e-mail and you've chatted with key pals around the world. So far, you and your friends have been the ones providing most of the facts and ideas. Where's all of that wonderful information that's supposed to be out there on the Internet?

An awful lot of it is clumped in a humongous collection of facts and fun called the *World Wide Web*. We dedicated a big chunk of this book to the World Wide Web (also called simply "the Web") because it's the best collection of stuff we know. This chapter gives you an introduction to the Web; Chapter 7 will get you started as an official Web crawler.

WHAT'S THE WORLD WIDE WEB?

Basically, the Web is a collection of information. You might think of it as a giant information mall that includes a library, magazine store, music shop, and video rental outlet.

A lot of different kinds of people and places publish information on the Web. They publish Web "pages." Here are just a few examples of different kinds of Web pages:

- a fourth-grade class publishes a Web page that describes and shows their current projects

- a toy manufacturer publishes a Web page that advertises its new products

- a science museum publishes a Web page that makes you feel like you're actually visiting the museum

- a TV network publishes a Web page that tells you all about TV stars and programs

- a kid in Nebraska publishes his own Web page that includes pictures of his family and his pet goose

- a government agency publishes a Web page that gives you information about the last census

- a teacher publishes a Web page that tells you her favorite Web pages

What else is on the World Wide Web? It might be easier to ask what isn't. People are publishing new stuff on the Web every day. Skim through Chapter 9 to get an idea of the different kinds of Web pages out there.

Web pages have a multimedia format. That means that they include more than just text. A Web page can include pictures, sounds, and even videos.

THE WEB VS. THE NET

The World Wide Web and the Internet are *not* the same thing. The Internet is that giant information highway, a zillion "roads" connecting computers around the world. The World Wide Web is a collection of places, or sites, that you can visit. Basically, you can think of the Web as containing the places you want to go. Of course, you need to ride the Internet to get there!

I'M FEELING HYPER!

One of the reasons that information is so easy and so much fun to use on the World Wide Web is that *you* control how it is given to you. You can do this because of something called *hypertext*. Hypertext lets you decide what you will look at, listen to, or watch.

Let's say you want to find out about mummies. You could go to the library and read a book about mummies. To understand the book, it'd be a good idea to start at the beginning and read the pages in order. If you start jumping around, you'll probably get confused. The information was designed to be read in order, from page one to the end.

If you're using the Internet, there's no set order. You might start out by reading an article on mummies published by a history museum. As you're reading the Web page, you're bound to see some words highlighted, as in this example:

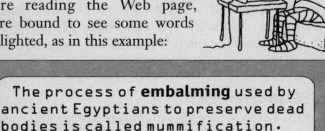

> The process of **embalming** used by ancient Egyptians to preserve dead bodies is called mummification. After death Egyptian pharaohs, such as **Amenhotep II**, were mummified and buried in elaborate **tombs**.

When a word is highlighted on a Web page, it means you can click on it and something will happen. In this paragraph, clicking on **embalming** might take you to a lengthy description of the embalming process. Clicking on **Amenhotep II** might show you a picture of the pharaoh's actual mummy. You might click on **tombs** to find out more about Egyptian burial places.

Of course, you can click on pictures and on buttons, too. All these tools are how hypertext lets *you* organize the information. You can read or watch whatever you want to. People who write Web pages design them to be as open and flexible as possible. Every visitor will use a Web page in a slightly different way. In fact, you can visit a really good Web page over and over again and never get bored.

Another big word for this is *interactive*. You hear a lot about interactive this and interactive that. All this means is that you, the computer user, get a chance to interact, or participate, in what's going on.

HOME AWAY FROM HOME

When you crawl around the World Wide Web, you'll be going from Web page to Web page. Web pages that are grouped together at a single URL are called a *Web site*. And most Web sites begin with a *home page*.

A home page is the first page you see when you visit a Web site. For example, suppose you want to visit the Web site published by the Smithsonian Institution. The first page you go to is the Smithsonian's home page. This page is like a table of contents. It tells you about the different kinds of information you will find at this Web site.

A WEB SITE

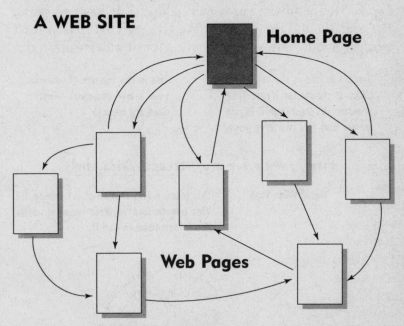

This diagram shows the organization of a Web site. You enter the Web site through the home page. Then you jump around to different Web pages, depending on what you click on and what you do. This diagram shows a very simple Web site. Most sites have a lot more pages and links. Even when there are hundreds of links, though, a good Web page is still easy to use.

AND YOU THOUGHT E-MAIL ADDRESSES WERE COMPLICATED . . .

So now you have some ideas about what you'll find on the World Wide Web. But how are you going to get there? Well, remember, every Web site really exists on some computer somewhere. The trick is telling your computer where the Web page you want is stored. That's why every Web page has a specific address. All you need to do is type in the address, and your Web browser will use the Internet to find the Web page you're looking for.

A Web page address is called a *URL*, or *Uniform Resource Locator*. Remember your e-mail address? It has two parts: the user ID and the domain. Well, every URL has at least two parts, but most of them have a lot of other stuff, too.

You'll see this at the start of most URLs. It stands for *Hyper Text Transfer Protocol* (ugh!). It just means that this is a Web page.

This is the domain. (Remember your e-mail domains? What does *org* mean?)

http://www.zen.org/~brendan/kids.html

World Wide Web

This is more information about where the Web page is located. Your browser needs this information to find it.

The address on page 58 gets you to The Kids on the Web, a great list of Web sites you might want to explore. Notice that the URL contains the letters *www*, for *World Wide Web*. A lot of URLs have these letters, but a lot don't. You can't just automatically type in www near the beginning of a URL and expect it to be right. In fact, when you're typing URLs, you need to be extra-careful.

URLs have to be typed *exactly* the right way, or you'll never get where you want to go. Look closely, and type what you see. A few points to remember:

• URLs never include spaces, commas, or semicolons.
• Some URLs contain a symbol called a *tilde* (~). You'll find it to the left of the 1 on your keyboard.
• There are two kinds of slashes on your keyboard. URLs use the one (/) that's below the question mark, not the one that slants in the other direction.

Even though the World Wide Web has sites all over the world, it doesn't have the same name everywhere. One newspaper in China translated World Wide Web into a phrase that means *Ten-Thousand-Dimensional Web in Heaven and Net on Earth!*

Chapter 7

Crawling Around the World Wide Web

So the World Wide Web is a surprisingly big collection of pages published by people and organizations all over the world. This chapter will help you find your way around the Web. You'll soon see that it's not hard to become a super Web crawler.

JUST BROWSING!

To use the World Wide Web, you need a kind of program called a *Web browser*. There are lots of Web browsers out there. Some of the best known are Netscape, Internet Explorer, and Mosaic. Services such as America Online and CompuServe have their own Web browsers.

Your Web browser is probably part of your communications software. Chances are it's already loaded into your computer. If not, ask someone for help.

To start browsing the World Wide Web, find the button for your Web browser and click on it. A new screen will appear—your Web browser screen.

FINDING YOUR WAY AROUND THE WEB

Take a look at your Web browser. Take a *good* look. All the tools and buttons you need to get around the World Wide Web are on the screen. You can point your mouse and click on a button to get around the Web, or you can type in a Web page address to go right to that page. You can also build a list of favorite spots on the Web that will take you back to your favorite places. If you *really* like a page, you can print it out and take it with you. All these options are found in your Web browser.

Title Bar **Address Bar** **Web pages show up here!**

Menu Bar **Tool Bar**

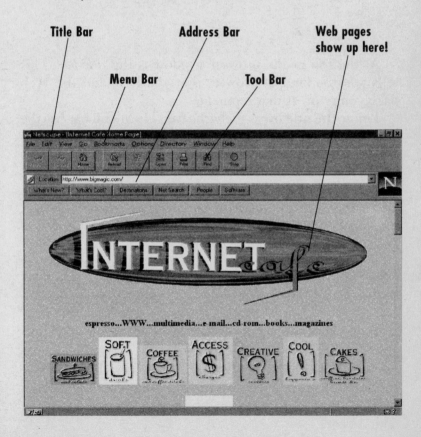

At the top of the browser window is the *title bar*. This tells you the kind of browser that you have and the Web page you're on at that moment.

Below the title bar is the *menu bar*. The menu bar has the File, Edit, and other tools for the browser. The menu bar will help you to navigate the Web, set up your printer to print Web pages, and create your list of favorite places. This list is called a *bookmark* or just a *favorite places menu*. You can mark your place on the Web just like you do in a book and come back to that place anytime. We'll show you how to do this later in the chapter.

Under the menu bar is the *tool bar*. This has pictures called *icons* on it. You click on icons to move around the Web pages, print a Web page, and look for things on the page.

Below that is the *address bar*. The address bar will show you the address of the Web page you are currently looking at. You know what the Web address is—the URL, or the location of the Web page on the Internet. No matter which browser you have on your computer, there will be an address bar.

You can go to other Web pages by typing the new Web page address (the URL) in the address bar. Try this now. Look up the address of a Web page from a magazine, a newspaper, or a TV program, or use this book. You'll find those pesky URLs hiding everywhere nowadays, even on breakfast cereal boxes, toy packages, and advertisements.

Once you've typed in the Web address, press the Enter key. The browser will now try to find the Web page at that address and show it to you on the screen. After a short wait (you hope), your new Web page will be up on your screen, in full color with pictures and everything. Easy! Except when something goes wrong, of course.

What can go wrong? Well, it's very easy to misspell the Web page address. If the browser shows you a message such as, "The Internet site 'www.Webpage.com' was not found. Please make sure the address is correct," go back and check the address. If it is correct, then the Web page might not be there anymore, or else the Web site the page is on might be disconnected from the Internet at that moment. This happens now and again on a network as big as the Internet. Try the address again later.

THE DREADED 404S, 403S, AND 500S

If the Web address you looked for is not found, you might get this error message on your screen:

```
404 Not Found
The requested URL was not found on this
server:
/pages/foo.htm
(E:/Website/htdocs/docs//pages/foo.htm)
```

This means that the address is not valid. The first thing to do is to check your spelling. If it's okay, the Web page you're looking for has probably moved to a different address on the Internet. Or it might be gone for good.

Another error message you might find is:

```
403 Access Forbidden
Access to the requested URL is not allowed.
```

Yipes! Does this mean you're a hacker and the police are on their way? No, nothing that extreme. It means that the Web address you gave is not accessible. Why? Well, maybe you have to be a member of a club or something. Anyway, you can't get in!

And another error message is:

```
500 Server Error
This server has encountered an
internal error which prevents it from
fulfilling your request.
```

This means that there is something wrong at the Web site. It's not you or your browser that did it, so try again a little later.

BE LIKE A DUCK—GET WEBBED!

Now you've got a Web page up on your browser screen. This page is called an *HTML document*. That stands for *Hyper Text Markup Language*. HTML is the language of the World Wide Web. All Web pages are written using HTML. HTML is what causes Web pages to look like they do and makes it possible for them to travel over the Internet.

As you know, every Web page is a multimedia interactive document. *Multimedia* simply means that there is more than one kind of thing on the page. A multimedia document includes both pictures and writing. It may also have sounds and moving pictures. You've probably been reading multimedia documents for a long time and didn't even know it! If you've ever used a CD-ROM, you have seen this type of document before.

Remember, *interactive* means that *you* can control the way information is presented. You do this by clicking on buttons and highlighted words. Clicking on these spots will take you to other pages on the Web. Buttons can also take you to sounds, pictures, or videos. On every page there are words and pictures that are highlighted—these are the links to other pages, sounds, and pictures.

How do you know when you can click on something? Highlighted words are usually pretty easy to pick out. But there's another important clue: your *cursor.* That's the little shape that moves around on the screen when you move your mouse. Usually, your cursor looks like an arrow, but when you move it onto a button, it might look different. So when you see your cursor change shape, you can be pretty sure you've found something to click on.

The World Wide Web has grown *a lot* in just a few years. In 1993 there were about 1,000 pages to look at on the Web. Now there are over 20 million Web pages! Experts predict that millions of new Web pages will soon be added to the Web *every month.*

SURFING THE WEB

You know what a Web page is and how to jump from page to page using interactive buttons. But maybe you got lost. That's okay! Everyone has lost his or her place on the Web at some time or other.

Luckily, it's pretty easy to find out how to get back. This is a job for your tool bar. The tool bar of your browser has buttons to help you find your way around the Web.

The most important tools are probably the *Forward* and *Back* buttons. When you go from Web page to Web page, your browser remembers the order. Think of a pack of cards. Every time you visit a new page, you add another card to the stack. You can go forward or backward in the stack with these buttons:

Click on this button to go back one Web page.

Click on this button to go forward one Web page.

Another tool is the *home page finder*. This is a button with a picture of a little house.

If you press this one, you'll go back to the home page for your Web browser. That's a good place to start any Web activity. Even if you get hopelessly lost on the Web, you can always find home with the click of a button.

GETTING OUT OF TROUBLE

Strange things can happen when you're surfing. Sometimes a Web page takes forever to show up, and sometimes it just never arrives. And sometimes you get a Web page that looks as if it were written on Mars. There are two buttons on your tool bar that can help you get out of trouble while you're surfing.

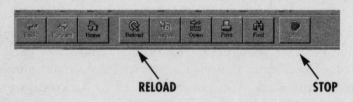

RELOAD   **STOP**

If your browser is looking everywhere, but no Web page shows up, press Stop to stop your browser from looking any further.

If a Web page shows up but looks like gibberish, try pressing Reload. It might help. If the page still looks weird, try another page.

SEARCH TOOLS

Now you know how to get around on Web pages. But how do you find things you're interested in on the World Wide Web? It's not that hard to find particular subjects on the Web. Remember, the Web is like a *really big* library.

You can use a special Web page called a *search service* to help you find what you're looking for. It's a hard job keeping track of millions of Web pages. That's what search services are for. These services are really just big lists, or indexes, of Web pages.

There are lots of search services, but they all work pretty much the same way. Here's how you locate a specific subject:

1. Look for a blank box on the Web page. That's where you type in the subject you're looking for, such as *dinosaurs* or *skateboards*.
2. Click on the Search button.

That's it! The search service will look through its list of pages and tell you where the word *dinosaur* shows up on the Web. It will display a list of Web pages you can go to. Just click on the name of a page to go right there. You don't even need to type in the URL.

Some search services, such as Yahoo and Infoseek, also let you browse Web pages by subject. These services have grouped Web pages into categories such as arts, government, or science. When you click on a big category, such as science, you'll get a group of smaller categories, such as astronomy and ecology. Once you pick a category you want to explore, the service will show you a list of Web pages for that subject. To go to the Web page, just click on the name of the page.

Every search service has its own list of Web pages. For example, you won't find every Web page on dinosaurs using only one search service. It's a good idea to use more than one service if you really want to know what's out there. Here's a list of some of the most popular search services:

AltaVista

URL: http://altavista.digital.com

excite by Architext

URL: http://www.excite.com

Infoseek Guide

URL: http://www.infoseek.com

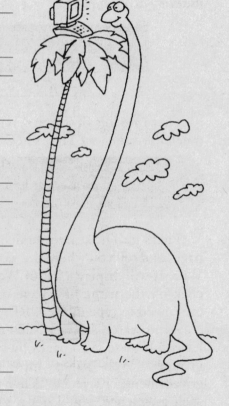

Lycos

URL: http://www.lycos.com

Magellan

URL: http://www.mckinley.com

WebCrawler

URL: http://Webcrawler.com

Yahoo

URL: http://www.yahoo.com

Skip ahead to page 84 to read more about using Yahoo to find topics.

PLAYING FAVORITES

Once you get to a really cool place, can you remember how you got there? That's a big job sometimes. You might be surfing through a museum and suddenly click over to a favorite book or game site. How can you get back to the museum?

On the menu bar is an option that lets you keep track of your favorite Web sites. Different browsers have different names for this option. It may be called *bookmarks* or *favorite places* or *hot list*.

When you're on a Web page you want to put in your address book, click on the Add to Bookmarks or Add Favorites option. That's all there is to it! The URL of the page you're on is now listed on the bookmark list. Whenever you want to go to this URL, just open the bookmark menu, find the spot you want to go to, and click. You're on your way back to a favorite place.

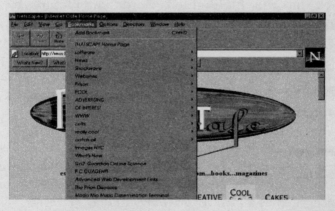

Keeping bookmarks of favorite places is a good thing for all Web surfers to do. You can build up quite a collection in a short time. Compare them with other people's lists, show them around, and trade favorite sites with your friends and e-mail pals.

COLLECTING STUFF WHILE YOU SURF

Just as you collect shells at the beach or rocks in the woods, you can collect cool stuff from the Web. You can find stories, sounds, pictures, videos, cartoons—even games—on the Web. Collecting and saving these things is called *downloading*, which simply means copying a file from another computer to your computer. It is the opposite of *uploading*, which is copying a file from your computer to another computer.

Downloading on the Web is easy. Point to what you want and click. The file will be copied from the Web computer to your computer without any problem. It's easy, and it's completely free, except for the time connected to the Web. The biggest problem is stopping. There is more stuff on the Web to download than you could ever fit on a million home computers!

When you find a page with something you want to have, click on the highlighted words or picture to start downloading. A message from your browser will ask you if you want to save the file. If you say yes, you'll need to tell your browser where to store the file on your computer. After you've named the folder and clicked on OK, the file will come down from the Web site and appear on your computer.

It's smart to keep all your downloaded files in the same place. Lots of Web surfers keep a folder called *Download* on their computers. Put everything you download into this folder. After you download, you can move it to another place, such as a *Pictures* or *Games* folder.

You'll sometimes need to use your own software programs to look at files you've downloaded. To view a picture, for example, try a picture viewer or paint program. To watch a video, try a movie player. To read a story, use your word processor.

Suppose you've downloaded a picture of a polar bear from a Web page. The picture is stored in a specific format. Some common formats are called *GIF, JPEG, PICT,* and *TIFF.* To view the picture, you need a picture viewer that can read the particular format the picture is stored in. Most picture-viewing programs can read a lot of different formats. To see your polar bear, just run your picture viewer, select Open, and locate the name of the polar bear file you downloaded.

Other files, such as games, need to be installed on your hard drive before you can access them. Be careful when you install anything on your computer. It's best to have help with this because the directions may be complicated. And there's another reason, too: *viruses!*

You may have heard of them: evil programs that can wreck your data. Viruses are hidden in programs. Any program may be infected with a virus. Some of these programs are on the Web. If you're not careful, you can infect your computer, and that can be big trouble. Ask your family or teachers to help with installing any program. It's better to be extra-careful than to catch a computer virus!

HELPER APPLICATIONS

Once in a while, you might find that your browser can't run something that's on a Web page. To hear a noise or watch a cartoon, you might need something called a *helper application*.

Helper applications are programs designed to help out your browser. For example, one helper application is called *RealAudio*. This program lets you play sounds while you're looking at a Web page. Other helper applications help your browser show animation or videos.

You can usually download these helpers when you find a Web page that needs one. There will be a button that says something like "Download RealAudio player." Click on the button, and you'll download the helper application you need. Remember, helper applications are programs, not data, so they may have viruses. It might be best to have someone to help you download and install new programs on your computer.

After you've installed the helper application, you'll probably need to follow more instructions. For example, you may need to tell your Web browser where to find the new helper you just installed.

Chapter 8

Five Fantastic Web Sites for Starters

With millions of pages to choose from, how can you decide where to go on the Web? Listed below are five fun and different Web sites that should give you some idea of what you'll find on the World Wide Web. Visit each site and snoop around a little. Then you should be able to branch out and explore the rest of the Web like an expert.

• **The White House** Find out more about the White House, the current first family, and the federal government.

• **The Great Adventure** Travel around the world without taking a step.

• **KidPub** Publish your own story, read stories written by other Internet kids, or collaborate on a group story.

• **The Kids on the Web** Explore a list of terrific Web pages just for kids.

• **Yahoo** Use a search service that helps you locate information on the Web about whatever topics interest you.

THE WHITE HOUSE

URL: http://www.whitehouse.gov

What's It About?

This Web site offers a terrific introduction to the first family, the White House, and current political topics. The *.gov* in the domain clues you in that this is a government site. Of course, the information on the White House page changes regularly. Political topics reflect current issues, and the first family changes at least every eight years!

What Can You Do?

From the home page, you are given eight choices of topics. You might use this page to find recent or historic presidential speeches. Or you might take a tour of the White

House. You can even sign your name in the electronic White House guest book. How many people do you think have visited this Web site? Check the guest book to find out.

The White House Web site has a section designed especially for kids. Click on the White House for Kids button to see what's there.

Special Features

• The White House Web site has many sound clips of presidential speeches. You can download a sound file and then play it back using a sound player. Or you may be able to use a helper application to listen to the speech while you're looking at the page. (See page 74 for more on helper applications.)

• In the upper left-hand corner of the home page, you'll see the words *[text version]* highlighted. You can click here to view a text-only version of this Web site. Text-only is a faster way to get information because it takes time to send graphics electronically. When you're in the text-only version, you can click *[graphics version]* to go back to seeing the full page with all its pictures.

THE GREAT ADVENTURE

URL: http://www.cmcc.muse.digital.ca/cmc/cmceng/childeng.html

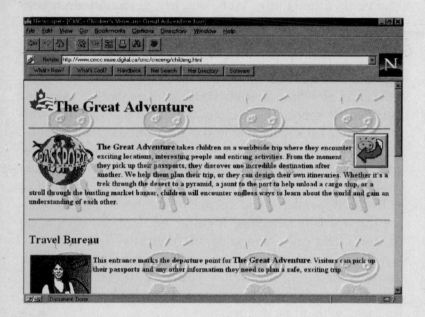

What's It About?

Travel around the world from one easy-to-use Web site. Based on an exciting exhibit at the Canadian Museum of Civilization's Children's Museum in Hull, Quebec, Canada, this Web page brings you an up-close look at many different parts of our globe.

Web Hunt

Look around and you'll find the answers to these questions.
- What direction does the Nile flow?
- How do you say Great Adventure in French?

What Can You Do?

Use the floor-plan map to decide where you'll go next in the exhibit. Display topics include deserts, communications, toys and games, and the Nile River, among others. Design your own plan of action as you find text and photographs for each topic you choose.

Special Features

• Like the White House page, this site can be used in a text-only version. That's helpful if you want the information quickly, or if your Web browser doesn't support graphics.

• This Web site is also available in a French language version. Click on the button that says *Français* to brush up on your French!

KIDPUB

URL: http://www.en-garde.com/kidpub/

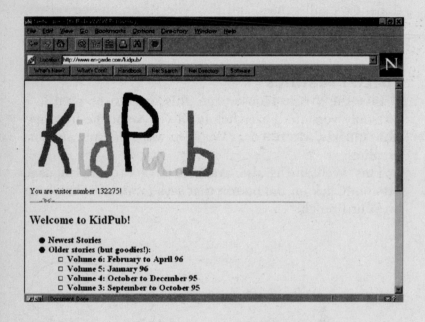

What's It About?

KidPub is a Web site designed to let kids share their own writing with other kids. Every day, kids from around the world add their stories and ideas to this site. It's a terrific way for you to publish on the Web.

Web Hunt

Can you find the answers to these questions at the KidPub site?

• What's a "Gary and Liz"?

• How many KidPub stories were read in Mexico? What about Taiwan?

What Can You Do?

Look at the KidPub home page. You'll see that you have a lot of choices. Here are your basic options:

- Read new stories by kids on the Net
- Read favorite older stories
- Add your own story to the KidPub site
- Contribute to a collaborative story written by kids from all over the Internet

Special Features

KidPub also has a special feature that lets you find out more about the kids who send in stories. Go to Statistics to find out how many kids are using this Web site and what they're doing there. Which stories are most popular?

It was a dark and stormy night...

THE KIDS ON THE WEB

URL: http://www.zen.org/~brendan/kids.html

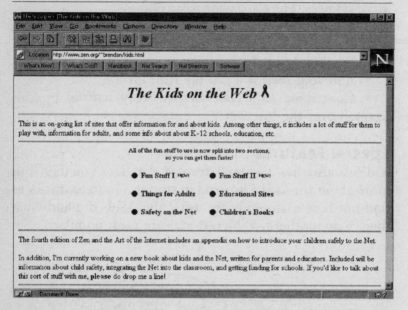

What's It About?

The Kids on the Web is a special kind of Web page. It's called a *links page* because it is a list of other Web pages that you might want to visit. Links pages are useful because once you get to the page, all you have to do is click on highlighted words to go to a new page. No more typing in those annoying URLs! There are lots of different links pages out there. You'll find more of them listed in Chapter 9.

Web Hunt

You can answer these questions as you take a look at Kids on the Web.

- What new sites are listed?
- Who creates this list?

What Can You Do?

This one could hardly be easier to use. All you do is look through the list and read the descriptions of Web pages. Find one that looks interesting? Click on the highlighted words—your browser will do the rest. Look at the URL line at the top of your screen. You'll see that the address has changed. That means you're at a new Web site.

After you've explored the page, you might want to return to the links page. Use the back arrow button on your Web browser tool bar to backtrack.

Most kids we know like to have at least one or two links pages in their bookmarks. When they sign on, they go right to their favorite links page. Many links pages, like The Kids on the Web, use symbols to show new entries. That'll help once you've explored the older links.

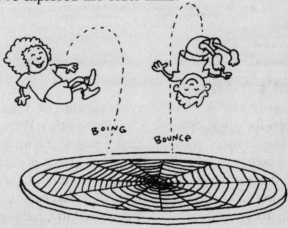

Special Features

The Kids on the Web is organized into sections to make browsing easier. You'll find Fun Stuff, Children's Books, Things for Adults, and Educational Sites. The New! icon highlights recent changes to this page. Check out these links to find the newest additions to kid's stuff on the Web.

YAHOO

URL: http://www.yahoo.com

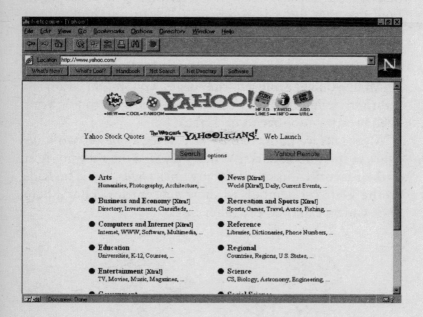

What's It About?

Yahoo is a Web search service. You'll recall that a search service helps you search the Web for specific words and topics. You'll find more search services listed back in Chapter 7, but Yahoo is a good place to start. It's easy to use and remarkably powerful. In just a few seconds, it can search thousands and thousands of Web pages to find just the topic you're looking for.

What Can You Do?

There are two basic ways to use Yahoo. The first way is to type in the specific word or phrase you are looking for, such as "Grand Canyon," "penguins," or "ozone." The second way is to browse through the categories listed on the Yahoo home page. Browsing is a terrific way to expand your knowledge of what's out there on the Web.

Finding a specific topic is easy as 1, 2, 3:

1. **Type the word or words you want to find (for example, "Robin Hood").**

2. **Click on the Search button.**

3. **Examine the search results.**

The search results will tell you how many entries were found containing your word or words. Each entry will have a separate heading and number. To go to a Web page, just click on the highlighted words.

Remember, you can type more than one word in the search box. If you type in a word that is really general, such as "computer," you might get thousands of Web pages back. It's better to type in a few words, such as "computer art geometric," to get a more focused list.

Of course, not every Web page will fill all your needs. If you're looking up penguins, some Web pages might be about Penguin-brand soda or household objects that look like penguins. You'll need to read the descriptions and visit different pages to find the exact information you want.

Special Features

At the bottom of the Yahoo home page, you'll find a list of other search services. After you've looked through the Web pages Yahoo found, try one of these other services. Because they all have unique lists of Web pages, another searcher will probably have some new places for you to look.

Chapter 9

Web Wildlife: An Explorer's Guide

This chapter tells you about a bunch of terrific sites on the World Wide Web. Take it with you to the computer when you're ready to start exploring.

> ## A few pointers before you begin:
>
> • Spell the URL *exactly* the way it's printed in this book. Remember, no spaces and no commas.
>
> • If you get an error message, try going to a different Web page. Come back to the first page later.

The Web sites in this chapter are organized in these categories:

• **Arts.** Includes fine art as well as art by kids (including you!)

- **By Kids/For Kids.** Web pages created by other kids

- **Entertainment.** Web sites with information about movies, television, music, and more

- **History and Social Studies.** Your ticket around the world and back in time—without having to leave your home

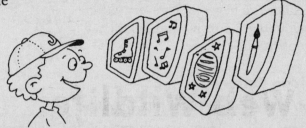

- **Links Pages.** Web sites containing lists of other Web sites—great for finding out about hot new sites

- **Reading and Writing.** On-line magazines or places to write your own masterpieces

- **Science and Math.** Really fun ways to find out more about these subjects

- **Sports and Recreation.** From Rollerblades to LEGO, lots of stuff about whatever ways you like to spend your free time

- **Other Cool Web Sites.** Weird stuff we couldn't resist

Really Important Point

As you know, some URLs are reeeeeeally long. In fact, some are so long that they wouldn't fit on one line in this book. When you see a URL that's broken into two lines, just type it all on one line. Don't add a space or anything else—just type the URL as it's printed here.

Aunt Annie's Craft Page

URL: http://www.coax.net/annie/annie.htm

Get step-by-step instructions for craft projects you can complete at home or at school. There's a new project every week, often including patterns and templates you can print out and use.

The Fridge Gallery

URL: http://www.ibm.com/Stretch/EOS/fridge.html

Here's another place for kids to share their art. The hosts promise that "it's unlikely that anything done by anyone over 12 will be hip enough for this gallery."

Lite Board™: Making Things with Light

URL: http://asylum.cid.com/lb/

Use colored pegs to create your own bright artwork, or view a gallery of artwork created by other users.

Web Museum Network

URL: http://www.emf.net/louvre/

Get inspired by viewing beautiful and famous works of art from the Louvre Museum in Paris, France. Special exhibits highlight specific artists; the general collection features some all-time favorites.

BY KIDS/FOR KIDS

Global Show-n-Tell

URL: http://emma.manymedia.com:80/show-n-tell/

At this site kids from around the world share their artwork on the Internet. Post your own favorites, or work with friends to create a collage.

Kids Did This!

URL: http://sln.fi.edu/tfi/hotlists/kids.html

This is a terrific links site that tries to keep up with all the exciting Web pages published by kids hooked up to the Internet!

Kids' Space

URL: http://plaza.interport.net:80/kids_space/

Here's a place for kids to meet and exchange ideas on the Internet. You might post your thoughts on a bulletin board, share your favorite drawings, or read stories written by other kids on the Net.

Mid-Link Magazine

URL: http://longwood.cs.ucf.edu:80/~MidLink/

Four times a year, a new issue of this magazine is published. Designed for kids in elementary school, Mid-Link includes topics of interest to kids everywhere.

Kids' Warner Brothers

URL: http://pathfinder.com/

Visit the home of Bugs Bunny, the Animaniacs, Pinky & the Brain, and more of your favorite characters. Get there by going to the Pathfinder home page and selecting Warner Brothers.

The Museum of Television and Radio

URL: http://www.mtr.org/

Reruns are an art form at this museum! Take an on-line tour of exhibits dedicated to preserving the best work done on TV and radio.

Radio Aahs On-Line

URL: http://pathfinder.com

Want to find out about a favorite TV or movie star? Or just curious about what other kids find entertaining? Check out this wild site by going to the Pathfinder home page and selecting Radio Aahs.

RARE: Ratings and Recommendations

URL: http://www.surf.com/rare/

Register at this Web site and rate your favorite movies and books. When you're done, RARE will recommend other movies and books you might enjoy, based on your ratings. You can look for TV shows, too.

Rollercoasters and Other Miscellaneous Insanities

URL: http://www.coasters.net:80/Coasters/

This is your Internet guide to rollercoasters and amusement parks around the world.

Teen Movie Critic

URL: http://www.dreamagic.com/roger/teencritic.html

Teenager Roger Davidson reviews current movies for you, with weekly updates.

HISTORY AND SOCIAL STUDIES

Abwenzi African Studies

URL: http://www.infosphere.com/abwenzi/

This group has been active since 1989, linking key pals in Aspen, Colorado, and Malawi, in central Africa. Follow the story of this fascinating collaboration in text and photos.

Gateway to Antarctica

URL: http//icair.iac.org.nz/

Find out more about the iciest continent at this *cool* Web site.

Kid's Window on Japan

URL: http://kiku.stanford.edu:80/KIDS/kids_home.html

Find out what it's like to grow up in Japan.

TIGER Mapping Service

URL: http://tiger.census.gov/

Sponsored by the U.S. Bureau of the Census, this Web site offers high-quality, detailed maps of almost everywhere in the United States. With version 2.0, you can even draw statistical maps using data from the U.S. Census. (Your Web browser needs to support tables for this option, but even if it doesn't, you can get great maps using version 1.3.1.)

The Vatican Exhibit

URL: http://www.ncsa.uiuc.edu/SDG/
Experimental/vatican.exhibit/Vatican.exhibit.html

This site offers facts, photos, and more about the history of Rome from ancient times up to today.

The Viking Network

URL: http://odin.nls.no/viking/vnethome.htm

Designed specifically for kids, this page based in Norway has lots of information about the Vikings, such as their travels and daily life.

World Surfari

URL: http://www.giaco.com/surfari/

Not too long ago, ten-year-old Brian Giacoppo of Phoenix, Arizona, thought up the idea for this terrific Web site. Every month, visitors find out about a different country. Where do you think you'll go today?

LINKS PAGES

Berit's Best Sites for Children

URL: http://www.cochran.com/theosite/KSites.html

Every site on this useful list is rated on a scale of 1 to 5. Use the ratings to help you decide which pages are really worth a visit.

Kids Places

URL: http://www.reedbooks.com.au/rigby /kids/kidplace.html

This is an awesome collection of places you've just got to visit!

Kids' Web

URL: http://www.primenet.com/~sburr/index.html

Here's another useful list of sites, updated regularly.

Kids Web

URL: http://www.npac.syr.edu/textbook/kidsWeb/

This great collection of Web sites is designed for school kids. The pages found here can really help you finish (or start) that research report.

Uncle Bob's Kids Page

URL: http://gagme.wwa.com/~boba/kids.html

Wow! This humongous collection of links will keep you busy for hours. It's organized into sections, so read the outline on the home page to get an idea of the links you'll find.

READING AND WRITING

Book Nook

URL: http://i-site.on.ca/isite/education/bk_report/booknook/

Book reviews by kids! Get ideas for what to read next, or add your own review to this growing collection.

Canadian International Penfriends List

URL: http://www.magic.mb.ca/~lampi/snailmail/ipl.html

You don't need to be Canadian to use this service and get a key pal to share your ideas with. You can register for free to get a list of 20 recent applicants or pay a fee and get a full list of applicants for the last three months.

Electric Postcards

URL: http://postcards.www.media.mit.edu/Postcards/

Here's new twist on e-mail! This page lets you send a postcard to your favorite key pal. Just find a picture you like from this on-line collection and send it to any e-mail address. Your friends will get a message saying that there's a postcard waiting for them at this URL. They'll also get a secret code number so that they're the only ones who can see your message!

Splash Kids Online Magazine

URL: http://www.splash.com/

This on-line magazine was created with kids in mind. Each issue has a special topic and includes contributions from real kids.

Web.Kids

URL: http://www.hoofbeats.com/

Want to try your hand at writing an exciting science fiction adventure? Enter this "off-world" story that you help to create!

SCIENCE AND MATH

Animal Information Resources at Sea World

URL: http://www.bev.net/education/SeaWorld/infobook.html

Take the Sea World Animal Information Quiz, or use this site to find out more about your favorite aquatic animals. How do they train whales to do tricks? Find out here.

Ask Dr. Math

URL: http://forum.swarthmore.edu/dr-math.html

Stumped on a homework problem? Is a number puzzle driving you crazy? Stop banging your head against the wall and sign on to this Web page. Dr. Math will send you strategy hints to help you solve even the hardest math problems.

The Exploratorium

URL: http://www.exploratorium.edu/learning_studio/

This is the on-line extension of San Francisco's famous science museum the Exploratorium. Visit electronic versions of favorite exhibits and follow links to other great science spots on the Net.

Mega-Mathematics

URL: http://www.c3.lanl.gov/mega-math/index.html

Can we really use the words *fun* and *math* in the same sentence? Sure we can! And you will, too, after visiting the colorful games and activities you'll find at this site.

Questacon

URL: http://sunsite.anu.edu.au/Questacon/

Go to the Kid's Place at the National Science and Technology Center in Canberra, Australia, to explore the current exhibits and activities.

Steve's Ant Farm

URL: http://sec.dgsys.com/antfarm.html

Yep, it's a real ant farm. Photos of the farm are regularly updated, so you can watch the progress as these busy little critters build tunnels, bridges, and caves.

You Can: Beakman and Jax's Web Site

URL: http://www.nbn.com/youcan/

Explore the world of science with Beakman and Jax. Get answers to 50 fascinating questions, download some wild sounds, or join a research project.

Everything Barbie®

URL: http://faoschwarz.com/barbietoc.html

Here you'll find fabulous outfits for Barbie, Ken, and their friends.

The LEGO Page

URL: http://legowww.homepages.com/

Pictures of amazing LEGO constructions, instructions for building your own, and even a LEGO theme song can be found at this site.

Sports Illustrated for Kids

URL: http://pathfinder.com

Get up-to-date information about your favorite athletes and sports in this on-line magazine. Go to the Pathfinder home page and select Sports Illustrated for Kids.

Web-a-Sketch

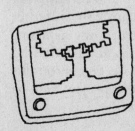

URL: http://www.digitalstuff.com/web-a-sketch/

Try this on-line version of Etch-a-Sketch. Enter your artwork in an ongoing contest, or view past winners.

OTHER COOL WEB SITES

Britannica Birthday Calendar

URL: http://www.eb.com/calendar/calendar.html

Find out who else was born on your birthday!

Cool Word of the Day

URL: www.dsu.edu/projects/word_of_day/word.html

Get a new word every day. Plus, submit your ideas for future cool words.

The Computer Museum Network

URL: http://www.net.org/

Sponsored by The Computer Museum in Boston, Massachusetts, this site offers an in-depth look at how computers work, as well as lots of on-line activities and exhibits that can help you become computer-savvy.

A Day in the Life of Cyberspace

URL: http://www.1010.org

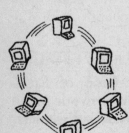

On February 8, 1996, people around the world participated in a giant Internet adventure. More than 250 different users were documented, from elephant-trackers in Malaysia to Inuit kids who live near the North Pole. Details on this ambitious time-capsule project can be found at this Web site.

I, Rearrangement Servant
(Internet Anagram Server)

URL: http://lrdc5.lrdc.pitt.edu/awad-cgibin/anagram

If you rearrange the letters in your name, what can you spell? The Internet Anagram Server can help you find out. Send any set of letters to this service, and you'll get an e-mail response back that gives you a list of anagrams.

Pet Pages

URL: http://www.dynamo.net/dynamo/pets/pets.html

See other people's pets, hear them bark or meow, or put your own pet on the Net for others to admire!

Wacky Web Tales

URL: http://www.hmco.com:80/hmco/school/tales/

Fill in the blanks, and the computer will write a wacky tale using your ideas. You'll be surprised how it turns out!

Joseph Wu's Origami Page

URL: http://www.cs.ubc.ca./spider/jwu/origami.html

View amazing photos of paper dragons, unicorns, centaurs, and more created by master paper-folder Joseph Wu. Or download patterns and instructions for creating your own Origami menagerie.

The World Wide Web Fortune Cookie Machine

URL: http://www.mind.net/sage/fortune/

PlaidMan's Fortune Server

URL: http://www.math.grin.edu/~leppik/cookie.cgi

Get a new fortune every time you go to either of these Web pages. At the World Wide Web Fortune Cookie Machine you can even add your own clever fortunes to the fortune data bank. PlaidMan's Fortune Server will show you a picture of a real fortune from a real cookie.

The Yuckiest Site on the Internet

URL: http://www.nj.com/yucky/index.html

We won't tell you what's here, but think *creepy crawlies* . . .

Chapter 10

Armadillos on the Internet: A Research Project Case Study

As you now know, the Internet is filled with an astonishing variety of information on a zillion subjects. Some of this information is just funny or weird, but a lot of it is really useful. That makes the Internet a wonderful research tool.

Suppose that your teacher gives you an assignment to write a report about a state in the United States that you have never visited. What would you do? Well, you could go to your school library and look up information in encyclopedias, magazines, travel guides, and other books. You could also ask friends and family members about states they have visited. Or you could sit down at a computer and use the Internet to find the information you need.

This chapter will give you some ideas about how to use the Internet to research a topic. Everyone uses the Internet in his or her own way. This chapter tells you how four kids used it to write a report. And it all begins with armadillos.

You met Jenny in Chapter 2. She and her key pals showed you some of the things you can do on the Internet. One day when Jenny walked into class, her teacher, Mr. Acevedo, had one of those looks in his eyes, the kind of look that meant he was going to give out an assignment that he thought would be really fun—but challenging.

Mr. Acevedo divided the class into teams. Jenny's teammates were Carla, Adam, and T. J. Everyone was waiting to hear what the project would be.

"Well, class," Mr. Acevedo said, sounding very pleased with himself, "since you've all gotten to know your way around the Internet, I thought I'd give you a chance to show off. I want each team to choose one topic, any topic, and find out everything you can about the topic—using the Internet."

There were some groans and whistles. Then the teams started making plans. Jenny's team decided to call themselves the Internauts.

Coming up with a topic wasn't hard at all. T. J. wanted to do something fun and kind of strange. Carla and Jenny agreed. Then Adam said, "Let's do a report on armadillos. How much information can there be on armadillos?"

Each team member set out to explore the Internet in search of armadillo facts. Here's what the Internauts found.

JENNY'S SEARCH

Jenny decided to start her search using Yahoo. She signed onto the Internet at her school computer lab and typed in the URL "www.yahoo.com." When the Yahoo home page showed up, she typed the word *armadillo* into the search box and then clicked on the Search button.

In just a few seconds, Yahoo found 22 different Web sites that mentioned the word "armadillo." But when Jenny started to read through the list, she realized something wasn't right. Here are some of the first entries Jenny saw:

Yahoo Search Results

Found 12 matches containing armadillo. Displaying matches 1-12.
Recreation:Animals, Insects, and Pets:Armadillo

Business and Economy:Companies: Computers:Peripherals:Printers
• Armadillo Software Corporation - State of the art software development using C++; OS/2, Win32, and Unix; specializing in software Internationalization (I18N).

Business and Economy:Companies: Computers:Software:Maps
• Aaarmadillo eMAP - Download share-ware that enables your own software to display a built-in map of sites, vehicles, and customers seamlessly.

> Business and Economy : Products
> and Services : Sports
> • Extreme Performance Armadillo
> brand Composite Skateboard

Wait a minute, Jenny thought. *These aren't about armadillos! They're just companies that use the word* armadillo *in their name. I guess it's interesting that there's an Armadillo brand skateboard, but that's not what our report's about.*

But then Jenny looked down the list of other Web pages and found just what she was looking for.

> • Armadillo Page - Uses For - If you
> have an armadillo and never know what
> to do with it, look here. A prize goes
> to anyone who has tried them all.
> • Home to the Armadillo - A tribute
> to Austin's favorite animal.

Jenny tried the first page. It turned out to be a weird list of 305 things to do with an armadillo. Funny, but not very useful. Then she found the Home to the Armadillo page, sponsored by a company in Austin, Texas.

This page gave Jenny a lot of great armadillo facts. She found out that they're related to sloths and anteaters and usually weigh about 8 pounds. Jenny saved this Web page so that she could print out the information and use it for the report.

ADAM'S SEARCH

Adam also used the computer lab at school. Jenny gave him the address for the Home to the Armadillo page, so he started right away by typing in the correct URL.

Jenny hadn't read the whole page, but Adam scrolled all the way to the bottom. There he found links to other Web pages.

His eyes lit up when he saw a link to a page called Armadillo Internet Resources! He clicked on the link and found a new list of more than 20 Web pages about armadillos!

Of course, a lot of these pages were about products or clubs that just happen to be called *Armadillo*. But several of the pages had new, fascinating armadillo facts. On one page Adam found out that an armadillo has two options for crossing a river. It can just sink to the bottom and walk across, or it can swallow air into its stomach and float across! Adam saved every page that had interesting information on it.

CARLA'S SEARCH

Carla was really excited about finding out about armadillos. Adam gave her the URL for the Armadillo Internet Resources page. When she got there, she saw an interesting link to a restaurant in Texas. The restaurant had a wonderful home page, with lots of beautiful pictures and some weird sounds. She couldn't find an armadillo anywhere, though.

At the end of the page Carla found some links to other Web pages. One of the links was to a Texas Board of Tourists page. Carla had always wanted to visit Texas, so she went to this page.

For the next half-hour, Carla found more and more interesting pages about Texas and Texas history. She read about the Alamo and the years that Texas spent as an independent republic. Then her time was up.

"Oh, no!" she cried, "I don't have any new armadillo information."

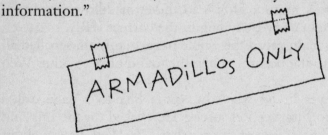

Carla got sidetracked. Chances are this will sometimes happen to you, too. It's hard to resist clicking on something that looks intriguing, and the World Wide Web is chock full of goodies. Unfortunately, your time is usually limited. So if you're doing a research project, try not to go to pages that you're pretty sure won't be very useful.

Carla decided to go back to the computer lab after school. She wrote a big sign for herself that said *Armadillos Only* and taped it next to the computer.

She found two terrific Web sites with more armadillo tidbits. Carla found out that armadillos can jump 4 feet straight into the air, and that they usually have litters of four identical babies. She also learned that armadillos were originally introduced into the United States from Mexico about 150 years ago.

Another page told Carla about a fascinating fossil discovery made in the Seymour Islands off Antarctica. Scientists recently discovered an ancient relative of the armadillo that was the size of a small car!

T. J.'S SEARCH

T. J. decided to try a different strategy. He likes to go to chat rooms and talk about his projects. So T. J. signed onto the Internet and went to his favorite chat room. His ID is TJTJTJ. Here's a bit of the conversation he had with some new key pals.

TJTJTJ: Hi, my name's T.J. I'm doing this report on armadillos. Has anybody ever seen a real one?

Xora876: No, but my sister looks like one.

Benina: In a zoo in San Diego.

Nomi200: I think they're cute.

TJTJTJ: Do me a favor and ask your friends if anyone ever met one for real. They can send me e-mail at TJTJTJ@wild.com.

T. J. went to three other chat rooms and asked if anyone had run across an armadillo in the wild. One kid thought she had seen one but admitted that it might have been a raccoon instead.

The next day, T. J. signed onto the Internet and found this message waiting for him:

To: TJTJTJ@wild.com
From: In2Netting@aol.com
Subject: Dillos!

I heard from my friend that you wanted stories about armadillos. My family and I found one in the wild about a year ago. It had a broken leg, so we took it to the vet. It had to wear a cast for a long time, so we kept it at home and fed it. If you want to know more, just send me an e-mail with your questions.

T. J. wrote a note to In2Netting right away, asking a whole list of questions about the armadillo. When the team got together to assemble their report, T. J. had a lot of interesting facts about In2Netting's particular armadillo, such as how it liked to have its head stroked, but only on the top, not on the sides. T. J. was pleased because he had found some facts that he might never have found in a book.

RESEARCH TIPS

The Internauts found information in a lot of different ways. Here are some tips to help you when you're using the Net for research:

• Yahoo is a good place to start, but remember that not all of the sites will be useful to you. Read the entries carefully to try to determine what kind of information they give.
• Some sites may not be on Yahoo. Look for links on other Web pages. Links are often found at the bottom of a Web page.
• Set a goal and stick to it. Try not to get distracted by Web pages that are funny but not all that useful.
• Use chat rooms and e-mail to get information from key pals.

Useless But Interesting

If you want to check out some of the armadillo pages the Internauts used for their report, try these sites:

Home to the Armadillo

URL:http://www.quadralay.com/Austin/Dillo/dillo.html

An introduction to all things armadillo

Armadillo Internet Resources

URL:http://spacely.dfci.harvard.edu/staff/Pelagatti/armadillo.html

A good list of links to armadillo pages on the Net

305 Things to Do with an Armadillo

URL:http://yan.open.ac.uk/~rogley/armadillo.html

A silly list that won't tell you much

Chapter 11

Playing in MUDs

You've learned a lot about how to use the Internet to find great facts and other kinds of digital information. Enough of that now! It's time to kick back and have some fun!

There are something like 12 gazillion different games on the Internet. Okay, that's an exaggeration, but you know what we mean. There are really simple games, like Tic-Tac-Toe, and games so complicated you could probably spend a year learning the rules.

This chapter will give you a brief overview of the different kinds of games out there.

MUDs, MOOs, MUSHes, AND OTHER STRANGE INTERNET LIFE FORMS

So, you're ready to play a game on the Internet, eh? Well, don't be a clueless newbie! Strap on your avatar and Telnet to the MUD nearest you! But watch out, don't get flamed!

Wait a minute! What are we talking about? Clueless newbie? Avatar? MUD? Are we speaking a human language? You bet we are! This is the language of games on the Internet, the language of MUDs. A *MUD* (that is, *multiuser dungeon* or *dimension*) is a computer program that you can log onto and explore. Each user on the MUD controls a computerized character called an *avatar*. With this avatar you can walk around, chat with other characters, explore dangerous (monster-infested!) areas, solve puzzles, and even create your very own rooms.

You can also get lost or confused if you jump right in, so be sure you know what you're doing before starting. It's a good idea to check out computer clubs at your school to find kids who know how to play MUDs already.

There are other types of MUDs, such as MOOs, MUSHes, UnterMUDs, and other varieties. If you want, try several different types of MUDs to see which you find the most interesting. If there's one thing MUDdom has, it's variety.

To play, you'll need to use a program called *Telnet*, which connects you to a MUD. Telnet is a program that connects one computer to another on the Internet. Only Internet users can get there—on-line services won't help.

It's not easy to use Telnet. You should probably get someone with experience to show you how to do it. Better yet, look over someone's shoulder while they play on a MUD. You'll learn a lot that way. Like we said, you can easily get lost out there. As a newbie, you could use someone with experience to teach you how to play in the MUD. A *newbie* is someone who has only recently begun to get into MUDs or really anything on the Internet. A *clueless newbie* is someone who gets into trouble when trying something new on the Internet, such as playing in a MUD.

It isn't a bad thing to be a newbie—we all begin as newbies on the Internet. A baby, after all, is the original newbie, and we were all babies once. Basically, you're a clueless newbie until you've got the hang of MUDding.

Bad manners or inappropriate behavior by newbies (or anybody) can result in the dreaded flame. A *flame* on the Internet is a message sent to someone about their bad manners or behavior. The best way to avoid the flame? Be nice, don't flame others, follow the rules. Then you won't get flamed.

We don't have the space here to tell you everything there is to know about MUDs and the other wild computer games on the Internet. Here's a Web site you can use to find out more:

Encyclopedia of MU##s Project

URL: http://www.eskimo.com/~hmcom/mud/wholedict.html

This is a dictionary of MUD, MUSH, and MOO terms.

OTHER GAMES ON THE INTERNET

There are lots of other games besides MUDs to play on the Internet. And there are plenty of games to download from the Internet and play on your computer. Some are very simple, like *The Skulls of Fate* at Dr. Fellowbug's Laboratory of Fun and Horror. Ask a "yes" or "no" question of the silly skulls on the page and get back a goofy answer. Other games are more complicated and can take days to play.

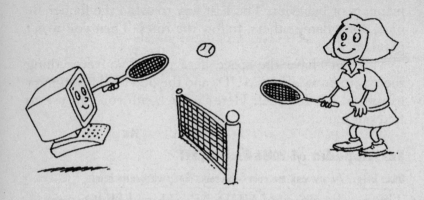

Here are some of our favorite games and game links:

AlphaWorld

URL: http://www.worlds.net/alphaworld/

This game is something really different on the Internet. It's more than a game—it's a lifelike world. After you download the game and install it, you can connect to AlphaWorld. Once there, you can scoot around the 3-D scenes complete with buildings and people. You can chat with the people, too. You can even build your own buildings and create your own cities if you want. You first get a piece of open land and use the game's building materials to construct a house or a palace. Plant a garden and put a fence around it if you like. This place can really pull you in. Once you're done building, you'll want to live there! There's a new Jumanji land inside AlphaWorld. Be sure to check it out.

BattleGate

URL: http://apt.usa.globalnews.com/battlegate/index2.html

This is a big, fancy, interactive game with characters, levels, and virtual fighting.

Connect Four

URL: http://csugrad.cs.vt.edu/htbin/Connect4.perl

This is a strategy game you can play against a computer. You can play it with full graphics or use a text-only version. (Text-only is good if you have a slow Internet connection.)

Cyber Jacques Cyber Seas Treasure Hunt

URL: http://www.cyberjacques.com/

Here's a great way to have fun and practice surfing the Web at the same time. Follow Jacques' clues to find information on the Web. Enter his contest to win real prizes, too!

Dig Zone

URL: http://ugWeb.cs.ualberta.ca/~hubick/digzone/digzone.cgi

Pick the monster you want to be, then dig your way through a maze of dirt, obstacles, and gold!

Dr. Fellowbug's Laboratory of Horror and Fun

URL: http:/www.dtd.com/bug/

Sounds, games, and other stuff for kids with a weird sense of humor. Try the daily noise (you never know what you'll hear next) or the excuse generator (perfect for when your homework isn't finished because you were surfing the Net!).

Fake Out!

URL: http://www.hmco.com/hmco/school/dictionary/

Do you know what a *hoplite* is? What does *ambrosia* mean? Try to pick the real definition out of a bunch of fakes sent in by kids on-line. You can send in your own fake definitions, too.

Gid's Games

URL: http://www.blueberry.co.uk/PIER-Gid.html

Gid's has lots of interactive games. Some are Web versions of familiar "real-world" games such as Tetris and Rubik's Cube.

Happy Puppy Games Onramp

URL: http://happypuppy.com

This site has shareware, freeware, and demos for PCs and Macintoshes. There are thousands of links from more than 1,500 pages. In addition to games, you'll find hints, solutions, game extensions, and programs that help you cheat on computer games.

Internet Gaming Zone

URL: http://www.zone.com/

Here you'll find various multiplayer on-line games, including bridge, hearts, and chess.

Kids' Crambo

URL: http://www.primenet.com/~hodges/kids_crambo.html

Join other Internetters who play word games such as Crambo, Piggy-Wiggy, and Doggerel. If you like words, you'll love these weird games!

John's Word Search Puzzles

URL: http://www.neosoft.com/~jrpotter/puzzles.html

Try to solve word-search puzzles in a wide range of subjects. (Hint: Save them on your computer and sign off the Internet before you start solving. It's cheaper that way!)

Manic Maze

URL: http://www.worldvillage.com/maze.htm

You'll get an on-screen prize when you can find your way out of this alien maze—if you don't go crazy first!

Shareware.com

URL: http://www.shareware.com/

A huge storehouse of programs of all kinds—games, utilities, you name it.

Tic-Tac-Toe

URL: http://www.bu.edu/Games/tictactoe

Can you beat a computer at this old favorite?

Web Hunt

URL: http://www.the-coast.com/fundaromix.html

Here's another treasure hunt game for cybersleuths!

Yahoo Internet Interactive Games

URL: http://www.yahoo.com/Recreation/Games/Internet_Games/Interactive_Web_Games/

This is a big list of Web gaming sites.

Zarf's List of Interactive Games on the Web

URL: http://www.leftfoot.com/games.html

If you're looking for games, this is another good place to look. It has direct links to the hottest games on the Web.

Chapter 12

Even More Cool Stuff on the Net

You've gotten this far. You must think, *I can send e-mail, chat, play games, and find out about everything from armadillos to zephyrs. There can't be more!* Well, there is—lots more. So much more that we could write another book about it. Before we go, we'll tell you a little about some of the other things you can hear, see, and do on that great big worldwide network, the Internet.

NEWSGROUPS

Newsgroups are groups of computer users who share a common interest, such as dalmatians, soccer, or comic books. You can think of newsgroups as chat rooms and e-mail combined into one. You write an e-mail letter (called an *article* in a newsgroup) and send it to the newsgroup list (called *posting*). Other people on the list (called *subscribers*) will comment or reply to your posting. All of the postings are sent around the Internet to all of the subscribers. Then it starts all over again.

There are over 14,000 newsgroups on the news system called *Usenet*, the biggest newsgroup system available on the Internet. Every newsgroup covers a different subject, so you should be able to find something that interests you here. But it takes a special piece of software called a *newsreader*, which is available free on the Internet. Some Web browsers, such as Netscape and Mosaic, include their own newsreaders. Get some guidance from other users before joining a newsgroup.

PUBLISH YOUR OWN WEB PAGE

Kids around the world are starting to publish their own Web pages. It's getting easier and easier to have your own "place on the Web." To create your own Web page, you still need some understanding of HTML—Hyper Text Markup Language—the language of the World Wide Web. HTML is not easy to learn. Fortunately, new software has been developed that will help you create a Web page without knowing HTML. These programs, which are called HTML editors, can do a lot of the work for you. For example, they can help you turn a document from a word processor into a Web page.

If you want to create your own Web page, you'll need four things:

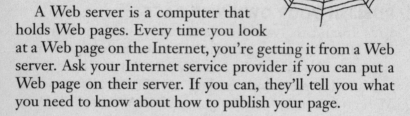

- **access to the Internet**

- **a word processor or HTML editor**

- **some knowledge of HTML**

- **a place to put your page, called a *Web server***

A Web server is a computer that holds Web pages. Every time you look at a Web page on the Internet, you're getting it from a Web server. Ask your Internet service provider if you can put a Web page on their server. If you can, they'll tell you what you need to know about how to publish your page.

Here are a few places where you can learn more about creating your own Web page:

Netscape Home Page

URL: http://home.netscape.com/assist/net_sites/index.html

This is a great place to start. Netscape is the program that started this stampede to the Internet in the first place.

Creating Your Own Home Page

URL: http://199.117.83.90/tutor/page7.htm

Creating Your Own Web Documents

URL: http://pen1.pen.k12.va.us/Anthology/Help/Mac/Creating.shtml

There are so many servers out there on the Web that we can't list them all. Search around and you'll find lots of information about making your own Web page.

NIFTY NEW STUFF ON THE NET

The Internet is changing every day. People are constantly thinking up new ways to make the Internet more exciting, more useful, and more fun. We thought we'd tell you a little about some of the exciting new trends in the Internet.

CU-SeeMe

URL: http://www.wpine.com/ins.htm

Imagine using your computer to see other people out there on the Internet and have them see you! With a video camera and CU-SeeMe, you can do that and more.

The software is free to use, and you don't even need a camera if you just want to look (or *lurk*, as it's called).

RealAudio

URL: http://www.realaudio.com/

Use the RealAudio player to hear tapes of radio broadcasts and music over the Internet. You won't have to wait forever to download sounds—just start the RealAudio player and you'll be listening to sounds on the Internet in seconds. This is a must-have for your Internet connection.

ShockWave

URL: http://www.macromedia.com

Plug this new toy for your Web browser into Netscape and see animation and videos and play games right on a Web page! A must-have for Netscape users.

Iphone

URL: http://www.vocaltec.com/

Now, in addition to chatting on the keyboard, you can talk to people all over the world on the Internet. With this product, your computer acts like a telephone!

Worlds Chat

URL: http://www.worlds.net/

Go to a world where you meet talking penguins, blowfish, and giant chess pieces. Cruise around this "world" as you float through cyberspace and chat using your keyboard. It's a thrilling experience

and a peek into the universe of virtual reality. And it's free—but it's pretty complicated to download and use. If you want to try, you'd probably better ask a computer whiz for some help (unless *you're* a computer whiz, of course!).

VDOLive

URL: http://www.vdolive.com

Watch live videos on the Web! This free software will allow you to view videos on your Web pages. It's almost—but not quite—like TV and looks cool on the Web.

Glossary

@ This symbol is used in e-mail addresses. It means "at" and separates the user ID from the domain.

attaching a file Add something to an e-mail message, such as a video.

chat rooms Also called chat lines. Electronic "rooms" where people talk to each other using their computers.

domain The part of an e-mail address that describes where the user's computer is located. Also, the part of a Web page address that describes where a Web page is stored.

downloading Copying a file from another computer to your computer.

e-mail Electronic mail, or notes that are sent from one computer to another using a modem.

hardware The physical parts of your computer system, including your computer, keyboard, monitor, and modem.

helper application A program designed to help or support your Web browser.

home page The first page you see when you visit a new Web site. A home page often acts as a table of contents for the Web site.

HTML Hyper Text Markup Language. HTML is the language of the World Wide Web. All Web pages are written using HTML.

hypertext Writing that is organized using links, so that a reader can jump from one piece of information to another by clicking on-screen buttons or highlighted words.

icon A picture or image on a computer screen which represents something. You click on icons to select something or open a file.

information superhighway A huge network of computers, all connected and passing information around the system.

Internet An interconnected computer network. Information from computers around the world travels on this network.

Internet Protocol (IP) The rules, or protocols, for addressing information on the Internet. Every computer on the Internet has an IP address. All information sent on the Internet uses IP addresses to get to the right place.

Internet Service Provider (ISP) A company that hooks you up directly to the Internet. Different from an on-line service, which goes through certain "gateways" to hook you up.

key pals Friends who meet on-line and talk to each other using their computer keyboards.

link A connection between two Web pages. You can click on a link to go from one Web page to another.

modem Your computer's telephone. Your computer uses a modem to connect to other computers, including those on the Internet.

MUD Multi-user dimension, a kind of role-playing game where players travel in imaginary worlds, or dimensions.

netiquette Rules that polite people follow when talking to each other in Internet chat rooms.

network A group of computers communicating with each other. The Internet is the world's largest computer network.

on-line Where you are when you are using the Internet. When you are connected to other computers through your modem, you are considered to be on-line.

on-line service A computer network that you can connect to, using your modem. The network is not connected directly to the Internet, but users can link to parts of the Internet from this network. America Online and CompuServe are examples of on-line services.

search service A Web site that helps you search for information in the World Wide Web. You can use a search service, such as Yahoo or Excite, to find Web pages about topics that interest you.

smiley A symbol used in e-mail or chat rooms to show emotion. Look at it sideways to see a face.

software The programs that run on your computer, such as word processors, database managers, e-mail, etc.

surfing the net Exploring different avenues or topics using the Internet.

uploading Copying a file from your computer to another computer.

URL Uniform Resource Locator. The address for a Web page. Every Web page has a URL.

user ID The name you are known by when you are on-line.

virus In reference to computers, a program written specifically to harm your computer or your data. For example, a virus might erase or jumble up all the information stored in your hard drive. You can protect your computer from most viruses by using antivirus programs.

Web browser A program that helps you navigate the World Wide Web. A browser, such as Netscape, includes a toolbar to help you move around the Web.

Web page A single page, or screen, in the World Wide Web. A Web page can include words, pictures, sounds, and video. The whole page may not fit on your computer screen. Use the scroll bar at the right of the page to see the top or bottom.

World Wide Web An enormous collection of electronic "pages" stored in computers around the world.

Index

America Online, 14, 24, 26, 35, 36, 48
ARPAnet, 25
avatar, 111

chat lines, 45
chat rooms, 18–19, 45–52, 108
 for kids, 18–19, 51–52
 saving a conversation in a, 51
 scrolling in, 50
CompuServe, 15, 35, 36
computerese, 23
connecting to the Internet, 36
cursor, 66
CU-SeeMe, 121

domain, 34–36, 58
domains, common, 36
downloading a Web file, 72

e-mail (electronic mail), 16–17, 33–44
 abbreviations, 43–44
 attaching a file to, 40
 body of an address in, 38
 header in, 38
 mailbox folder, 39
 personal address book for, 41
 Reply option in, 39
 saving, 39
 sending, 38
 why send, 33
 your first message on, 37–38
e-mail addresses, 34–36, 37
Encyclopedia of MU##s Project, 113
error messages (on the Web), 64

flame (on the Internet), 112–113

games (on the Internet), 21–22, 111–117
GIF format, 73
Great Adventure Web site, 75, 78–79

helper applications, 74
 viruses in a, 74
home page (on a Web site), 57
 creating your own, 119–120
 finder, 67
hypertext, 55
Hyper Text Markup Language (HTML), 65, 119–120
 document, 65
 editors, 119–120
Hyper Text Transfer Protocol, 58

icon, 14
information superhighway, 8
Infoseek, 69
installing your software, 16, 26

interactive, defined, 56, 65
Internet
    avoiding risks on the, 10–11
    chat rooms on the, 18, 48–52
    connecting to the, 26
    information flow on the, 31
    e-mail on the, 16–17
    friends on the, 10–11
    games on the, 22, 111–117
    how to get onto the, 23–30
    misunderstandings about the, 9
    modems for the, 23
    newsgroups on the, 118–119
    original name of the, 25
    picking password for, 29–30
    research tips for using the, 110
    researching a topic on the, 101
    software for the, 23
    what is the, 7–8
    what isn't the, 9
    World Wide Web on the, 20–21
Internet Protocol (IP), 30
    address, 30
Internet Service Provider
    (ISP), 24–25
Iphone, 122

JPEG format, 73

key pals, 13, 51
KidPub Web site, 75, 80–81
Kids on the Web site, 75, 82–83

links (to other Web sites), 57
links page, 82
    on the Web, 93

modem, 23
MOOs, 112, 113
Mosaic, 60

MUDs, 22, 111–113
MUSHes, 112, 113

"Net," the, 8
Net surfers, 10
netiquette
    defined, 50
    rules, 50
Netscape, 120, 121
network (computer), 7
newbie, 111, 112
newsgroups (on the Internet),
    118–119

on-line
    abbreviations, 43–44
    defined, 9
    friends, 10–11
    services, 24–25, 36
    shorthand, 44

paint program, 40
password, 10, 15, 29–30, 50
    picking your, 29–30
PICT format, 73
picture-viewing program, 73
Prodigy, 24, 35, 36, 48

RealAudio, 74, 121
RIPs, 12

search service, defined, 20
search services, 69–70
    popular, 70
ShockWave, 121
smileys, 42–43
software, defined, 23

Telnet, 112
TIFF format, 73

tool bar, 61, 62

UBIs, 12
Uniform Resource Locator (URL),
    49, 51, 57, 58–59, 62, 63, 71
    defined, 58–59
UnterMUDs, 112
uploading a Web file, 72
URL see Uniform Resource
    Locator
Usenet, 119
user ID, 14, 15, 27–30, 35

VDOLive, 122
viruses (computer), 73, 74

Web address, 62, 64
Web browser, 58, 60–63, 65
    address bar on the, 62
    bookmarks on the, 62, 71
    defined, 60
    favorite places menu on the, 62,
        71
    Forward and Back buttons
        on the, 67
    home page finder on the, 67
    hot lists on the, 71
    icons on the, 62
    menu bar on the, 62
    Reload button on the, 68
    Stop button on the, 68
    title bar on the, 62
    tool bar on the, 62
Web pages, 54–55, 65–70
    adding to address book, 71
    highlighting on, 56
    publish your own, 119–120
Web server, 120

Web site, defined, 57
Web sites, 75–85, 86–100
    arts, 88
    by kids/for kids, 89
    categories for, 86–87
    entertainment, 90–91
    five fantastic, 75–85
    history and social studies, 91–92
    keeping track of, 54
    links pages on, 93
    other cool, 98–100
    reading and writing, 94–95
    science and math, 95–96
    sports and recreation, 97
Web surfing, 10–11
White House Web site, 20, 75,
    76–77
World Wide Web, the, 20–21,
    53–100
    chat rooms on the, 49, 51–52
    Chinese translation of the, 59
    error messages on the, 64
    exploring the, 65
    highlighted words on the, 56
    home page on the, 57, 67
    HTML document on the, 65
    hypertext on the, 55–56
    organizing a site on the, 56
    publishing your own page on
        the, 119–120
    search services on the, 69–70,
        84–85
    vs. the Net, 55
    what is the, 54
Worlds Chat, 122

Yahoo, 75, 84–85, 103